"Abortion may well be the [illegible] over the past fifty years. Its impact goes beyond physical life to include emotional, spiritual, and relational devastation. *Healing the Hurt that Won't Heal* is the most comprehensive, biblical, and spiritually-informed book I've ever read that seeks to address the pain of abortion and point the way forward, heart by heart and soul by soul. This book is the perfect read for men, women, parents, pastors, and small groups who will muster the courage to face an ugly reality while committing themselves to God's grace-based solution and healing."

—**Gary Thomas**, author of *Sacred Marriage* and *Cherish*

"Having known Karen Ellison as a personal friend for over 20 years, I cannot count the number of times and ways I have been blessed by her consistent Biblical wisdom, guidance, prayers, and gracious heart of compassion. There is no one more called or equipped than Karen to lead this generation of abortion-wounded toward the healing every heart desires. Being abortion-wounded is either your story or the story of someone you love. *Healing the Hurt that Won't Heal*, is the book for all of us. It's time for those in hiding to be healed, and this is the book to guide the way."

—**Angela Thomas Pharr**, author of *Do You Think I'm Beautiful? Brave – honest questions women ask, Finding Hope in Fragile Places*

"Karen Ellison is the founder of Deeper Still which is a high impact post abortion healing ministry that effectively addresses the devastating impact of abortion on individuals and their families. In this book you will be inspired to action as you experience the transformational testimonies of men and women telling their stories of how Christ healed their abortion wounded past. It will promise to be a primary help for those who have never gone through an abortion to understand your neighbor (literally millions of people in our world). This is a must read for all pastors and ministry leaders!"

—**Kurt Dillinger**, Founder & President of LIFE International

Healing the Hurt that Won't Heal

Freedom for the Abortion-Wounded and Help for the Church They Fear

KAREN A. ELLISON

HIGH BRIDGE BOOKS
HOUSTON

Healing the Hurt That Won't Heal
by Karen A. Ellison

Printed in the United States of America
ISBN (Paperback): 978-1-946615-71-8
ISBN (eBook): 978-1-946615-30-5

High Bridge Books titles may be purchased in bulk for educational, business, fundraising, or sales promotional use. For information please contact High Bridge Books via www.HighBridgeBooks.com/contact.

Published in Houston, Texas by High Bridge Books

Cover photo credit Amy S. Traxler

Deeper Still
P.O. Box 11351
Knoxville, TN 37939
Book@GoDeeperStill.org

Dedication

To my beloved husband Arthur who loves me and blesses and releases me to God's calling on my life.

Contents

Acknowledgements

"Thank you" doesn't begin to touch the gratitude I feel for all the friends, family, and co-laborers who encouraged me to see this book through to its ordained purposes. I can't begin to name all the people who have prayed me through this project. You know who you are, and your names should be on this book as much as mine.

Thank you to those of you who allowed me to share portions of your story in this book– your sorrows and your victories. Those of us who've had the privilege of lowering you down through the roof to get you before Jesus will never forget those moments of grace when the veil of Heaven was pulled back and we watched as our kind Savior called your name and rescued your heart with His resurrection power.

I also must acknowledge all our children in Heaven. We live in the peace that we have been spiritually reconciled and in the hope that eternal relationship with them is just around the corner.

All the glory for this book goes to Jesus Christ. There would be no *Healing the Hurt that Won't Heal* if it wasn't for Jesus. He rescued me and gave me a voice so that His invitation could find you.

Introduction

Deep Things in Deep Waters

I'VE ALWAYS LOVED looking at water, whether a pond, lake, river, or ocean. There's something about water that's mesmerizing. It's mysterious and simple, and it can be dramatic and yet peaceful. People will often pay top dollar to have a waterfront view rather than to be landlocked.

I think one of the reasons for this is that it's safe to look at water. You can enjoy it vicariously. You can stare at it and be inspired by it all from the safety of your balcony, boat, or beach chair. It's something you can touch with your soul without having to get your toes wet.

When I was a child, I took swimming lessons. I liked the idea of being able to swim . . . until I got down to the lake and had to step into the cold, murky water without knowing how deep it was or what I might step on. The instructor would try to coax me in by reassuring me that I could trust him.

Eventually, I did learn to swim, but I was still very aware of my limitations. I would never be a strong swimmer. I could rescue someone in the confines of a swimming pool; however, my confidence ended there. If you wanted to venture out into open water, you were on your own.

After I finished college, I lived in Virginia Beach for several years. Living near the ocean, I took every opportunity I could to go walk on the beach. I could become totally immersed in the wind, the waves, the salt smells, the seagulls, the sandpipers, the crabs, and the sand in my toes. When I walked along the beach, all the sounds of other people, airplanes, or cars faded into the background.

I knew that ocean waves and currents were nothing to mess with, so I never ventured too far into the water. I never went out over my head—I went just far enough that I had to stand on my toes. The only thing that tempted me to swim farther was the occasional pod of dolphins that would come close to shore. I presume they came in to feed on something, but it seemed as if they were teasing the onlookers, inviting us to come and play. But even in the presence of all that playfulness, I had an underlying fear, because I knew I was in the presence of magnificent creatures God had made for the deep. They were strong and sleek, and they could be dangerous. They seemed to know who they were and what they were created for. I wanted to swim with them and learn what they knew about the God who had created them for deep places.

In my life, God has always revealed Himself through His creation and through the natural order of the things He set into motion. Even as I observe things going on around me in the outside world, the Holy Spirit, who lives in me, connects the dots for me and brings understanding to the spiritual principles of God's Kingdom. There are always spiritual lessons to be learned through this natural world.

One of the attributes of God that makes Him such a good and endearing Father is that He teaches us how to grow and trust Him step by step. And, with each baby step we take, He delights in our trust, our obedience, and our progress. Because God is rich in mercy and abounding in lovingkindness, He has the willingness and the ability to take our sinful choices as well as those sinful things done to us by other people and weave them together in a redemptive, miraculous, and beautiful way that reflects the deep work of God. This is what sets God apart from all the other gods of men.

One time when I was praying with a young lady who had been sexually abused as a young girl, the only way she could experience her own heart was like "shattered glass in a million hopeless pieces." As we began to pray and ask the Lord to bring light and healing to this devastation, He showed her a picture in her mind's eye. He was picking up each of those pieces of shattered glass and making a glass mosaic that was more beautiful, deep, rich, and reflecting of Him and His glory than she could have ever fixed or fathomed on her own. He was showing her what He was capable of doing—but it would require her to take steps of faith. It would mean walking through some painful places and being willing to swim out into the deep with Him.

Unless we are willing to venture into the deep, we will build our whole life in the shallows. We all start in the shallows. The shallows are a safe provision from a tender and wise Heavenly Father who knows our weaknesses and does not despise them. But if we stay in the shallows, we will never know or relate to our Heavenly Father beyond how a baby knows and relates to his father. You will know His safety and His provision, but you will never know the height, and depth, and breadth of His love, His sacrifice, His redemption, His pleasure, or His adventure.

My husband and I have a real estate investment on the Big Island of Hawaii, so we go there twice a year. The Pacific Ocean around the Hawaiian Islands is not like the ocean on the shores of a continent. Being on the Hawaiian Islands is like being out in the middle of nowhere, surrounded by a vast ocean. You're basically at the mercy of whatever atmospheric and oceanic conditions are in play on any given day. If there's a tsunami, you can only go so far inland until you're back at another shoreline. There's something wild and wonderful about all that, but the thing that captures me the most when I'm on this island is the water and its colors.

The ocean water that surrounds the Hawaiian Islands is clear. It's not murky or polluted, it just has a beautiful clarity. The colors are magnificent. The color of the ocean changes the farther out you go and the deeper the ocean floor gets. But even more amazing is that you only perceive the color change when the sun is shining and its light is refracting off the water. It's truly spectacular! It was the spectacular colors of the waters off the Hawaiian Islands that inspired the logo for the ministry I founded, *Deeper Still*, which I will share more about throughout this book.

I've never snorkeled much. I hate when water gets in my ears, and I easily get motion sickness, but beyond that, I have discovered that snorkeling is risky. Not only do you need to exercise safety, but there's always more to see the further out you go. You can get so caught up in the wonder of what you're seeing that before you know it, you look up and you're a long way from shore. And, at least for me, the farther out from shore I am the more fearful I become. I then determine that I want to work my way back to the shallows where I have the physical strength and stamina to get back on my own. I'll expend all my energy to get back to the shallows with the fishes, sea creatures, and coral that I've come to feel safe around.

What's wrong with that you might ask? Exactly! I ask the same thing—especially when something inside me looks out toward the deep. I start to regret that I came in so quickly. Why can't I just stay content here among my sea companions in the shallows? What keeps calling me out to those deep places to swim with the big fish—to explore depths of beauty and adventure I've never seen or known before? There comes a point when you swim out into deep waters that everything changes. The water gets colder, the fish get bigger, and the color of the water becomes deep, deep, blue. Somehow that all feels out of control, wonderfully out of control, but still out of control.

When God is drawing me to deep places, in Him, that's exactly how I feel. And I think that's exactly where He wants me—where He wants us, *all* of us. He made us to be creatures of the deep. Humans are made in the beautiful and amazing image of God! We are indeed fearfully and wonderfully made! He created us to know Him deeply. Those of us who know Him now (in this earthly life) will not fully know Him until we see Him face to face, at His second coming. But until that day, He has placed that longing in us to know the depths of our God, our Creator, our Heavenly Father, our kind Savior, our in-dwelling Holy Spirit, our Bridegroom, our Healer, our Comforter, our Eternal God who is both Lord and Friend.

For us image bearers, it's like God placed in us a homing device that He didn't put in any of His other creatures. In Ecclesiastes 3:11 we read that He has placed eternity in the hearts of men. And as expressed through the psalmist in Psalm 42:7, "Deep calls to deep at the roar of your waterfalls;

all your breakers and your waves have washed over me." How gloriously unique and crafted we are by the hands of a personal God who longs for deep fellowship with us, His image bearers!

I hope through reading this book you will feel the allure of your Heavenly Father who wants you to know Him in the depths of your soul and who is inviting you to trust Him through the deep waters of cleansing, healing, and restoration. The depths of God are fathomless. He is deep and He is wide and He is the creator of the universe, but best of all, He extends His hand to us and says, "Take my hand. I know you, I created you, I can save you, and I can heal you from the wounds that are too great for you to bear."

He will always call us deeper still. It is only when our spirit is awakened and—as the Bible teaches—born again that our spiritual "homing device" is activated and can hear the invitation to come out into the deep and have fellowship with the one we will adventure with for all of eternity.

No matter where you find yourself on your healing journey, you're still within the reaches of God's hand and His mercies. He does not despise shallow beginnings, but He will always beckon you to come away and trust Him to take you into deep places of His love and healing—places you only ever hoped for in heaven.

My prayer is that this book will serve at least two purposes. First, if you have an abortion-wounded heart, my hope is that you will hear the invitation of Jesus Christ. He is willing, able, and wildly passionate about redeeming and restoring your broken heart. You would not have this book in your hands if He did not place it there. His intent is to convince you that His grace and mercy is great enough for you, and that there is no more powerful or authoritative substance in the universe than His blood that was shed for you and for me on the cross. He is enough, and He wants to take you deeper still in knowing the mysteries of His love and the redemptive destiny He has for you.

Second, I pray this book will equip and awaken the Church to recognize the abortion-wounded world we live in. I want to summon you as a Christian or a church leader to awaken and allow your heart to be broken and emboldened by the devastation that sacrificing our children has brought onto this world. It has opened the door to every possible kind of evil. We are the end-time church, and it is our time and our watch. We have been commissioned to help the Bride make herself ready for the return of her Bridegroom. Revelation 19:7 says, "Let us rejoice and exult and give Him glory, for the marriage of the Lamb has come, and His Bride has made herself ready."

Throughout this book, I'm going to share different experiences, testimonies, and understandings I have gained through the ministry I founded called Deeper Still, www.GoDeeperStill.org. Deeper Still is a weekend healing retreat. Its purpose is to bring healing and lasting freedom to abortion-wounded hearts. As an organization, Deeper Still is now reproducing Deeper Still chapters in the United States and with international affiliates.

Within the following chapters, I have included some healing exercises, reflective questions, or action points to help you think through the issues raised in that chapter. If you have an abortion-wounded heart, I especially want to encourage you to open your heart to receive healing even through the reading of this book and doing the exercises. *But here's my caution* – This book and the healing exercises are not meant to be a substitute for attending a weekend retreat.

I believe the deepest levels of healing and freedom happen within the whole context of a retreat setting and environment. Depth of healing is best received in a Christ-centered community. The participants in a Deeper Still retreat richly benefit from a multi-gifted ministry team where each team member brings a piece of their healing. The body of Christ, when operating as a unified team, is the best conduit for the healing power of Christ. If you feel prompted to attend a Deeper Still retreat, I encourage you to do so.

For those who minister to the brokenhearted, remember this—The gospel (the good news) of salvation, healing, and restoration is not some esoteric, complex, unattainable, mysterious formula that only a few can grasp or minister. The Holy Spirit was sent to equip us, empower us, and release us to do the work of the Kingdom. We have the tools and we have the power. The only thing we bring to our commission is our *yes*, and it is a long and arduous yes.

To partner with the Savior of the world to bind up the brokenhearted, proclaim liberty to the captives, and set the prisoners free is an awesome adventure! It's dangerous though, and the sacrifices are great. When you venture into the deep with Jesus, He also shows you the broken places in your own heart. You see, the Kingdom of God is a level playing field. We all need to both receive and give from the same well of grace and mercy. As you read the pages of this book, I invite you to go deep, be courageous, and expect Jesus to take you deeper than you ever imagined you were capable.

A Preface to My Abortion Story

As a starting point to this book, I thought it necessary to include my own story about my abortion and how it affected my life. But not only how it affected my life, but how the Lord's healing presence changed the trajectory of everything in my life. Through my healing journey, I not only received His healing touch but, even more precious than that, I got more of Him.

I acknowledge that my story is from my perspective and so it has inherent limitations, but I pray that whatever is profitable to share will be clear and helpful. Because of the devastating effects of sexual sin and abortion, I am compelled to be open and honest about how I experienced this journey. Bringing things into the light is only profitable when it is redemptive, so my prayer is that you will see God's redemptive thread woven throughout this tapestry.

There are three key people who are an integral part of this story, and I could not tell it with full integrity if I did not include their influence in my life as it pertains to my abortion—they are my former boyfriend, my mother, and my father. Over the years, we've all taken steps to completely forgive each other and be reconciled with each other. I honor them for the painful journey they too persevered through to find peace and healing.

The power of the gospel is that we have a before-and-after story to tell. The redemptive purpose in sharing a testimony is not to expose people and their sins. Instead, we are to expose the enemy and his lies. But it's also to issue a warning to the deceptive nature of our own flesh. We can rationalize anything if we are left to our own thinking and fears. The key people of influence in my story have all been completely washed and covered in the blood of the Lamb.

Just see us as messengers wanting to spare others from similar pitfalls.

My story is not an extreme story of pain and suffering. In fact, my story is a common one—at least in the context of an American woman at the end of the 20th century. Perhaps the Lord chose me to share my story and the things He has taught me, because almost anyone can relate to some part of my story. If we imagine that all abortion stories are a result of extreme circumstances and abuse, then we may conclude that only the extremely wounded need a savior.

I refer to myself as one you would not have considered at risk for having an abortion, and I often wondered how I ended up here. So perhaps the redemptive purpose of sharing my story is to highlight the vulnerabilities we all share. We all need firewalls built into our lives to save us from ourselves and from the prowling lion. My prayer is that you would allow the Holy Spirit to help you see warning lights on the dashboard of your own soul so that you can shore up yourself and put those firewalls in place.

Since I have begun to write this book, my father has passed away and is now in the presence of the Lord. I have confidence he is now able to see the things of this life fully from God's perspective and has started his relationship with the grandchildren he never got to know here on earth.

Since my Dad's passing, I've been able to talk more in depth with my mother regarding the time surrounding my abortion and about that day itself. What a wonderful experience that has been. I heard things from her heart that I've never heard before that opened more wells of understanding and healing. I was also able to minister to her in deeper ways. I don't know why it's taken this many years for us to say and hear certain things, but these are now treasured memorial stones in our hearts. The Lord has poured out His grace on us in a way that has satisfied our hearts cry to know and see and feel what we needed to share about our family loss. We can now rest in that grace until we no longer see dimly as in a mirror but when we will see all things in the light of His eternal light and love. I will insert some of these recent disclosures as I recount my story.

In the last couple of years, I believe the Lord revealed to me that I had been pregnant with twins, a girl and a boy. This new revelation has been sobering but has also brought relief. There was an unrest in my heart that is now settled and at peace. As I share my story, I refer to my aborted children (my twins), but during those years, I only had a conviction about one child being aborted.

1

My Story: The Abortion Bomb

I HAD AN ABORTION in January 1981 in Pittsburgh, Pennsylvania. I had just turned 22 and was in a time of transition and uncertainty. I think if you had examined a profile on my life you would not have concluded that I would be at risk for a crisis pregnancy or an abortion, but therein lies the danger of conjecture from a profile. From my perspective though, I never saw this coming.

I was born and raised in Northwestern Pennsylvania in a rural farming community. I had a good and stable family life with Christian parents who imparted Christian values to their children and raised us in a good church. During our childhood in the 60s and 70s, we also had many opportunities to have our spiritual lives nurtured through youth camps and conferences. Even though no one has a perfect home life, family, or church community I felt I was blessed by what I had, and it was enough to give me a good start in life.

By the time I went to college, I felt grounded in my convictions about God, right and wrong, and black and white—at least morally speaking. Throughout high school, I was never too enticed by the party culture of some of my friends, so I avoided most of those pitfalls. When I first entered college, all those vices were present in bigger and darker ways, but the allure did not suck me in, thankfully.

Life changed for me though when I transferred to a Christian college. It was an amazing experience from the beginning, and I loved everything about it. I was hungry to learn more about the Bible and to grow in my walk with God. But the most amazing blessing to me was the fellowship of other believers who were also my peers. This was a new experience for me to have peers who were also new adults and who were living out and growing in their faith because they were choosing it instead of someone else choosing it for them.

Life in my new Christian community became a place of refuge, adventure, and trust. I felt I could finally let my guard down from always being assaulted by the empty, superficial ways of the world. I now had friends (not to mention professors) who were like-minded, like-hearted, and Kingdom focused.

Now, if this were a musical, the score would begin to change and you would hear a subtle bass undertone begin to emerge. About a year into my time there, I became friends with a guy who had a heart for God and amazing creative talent. His conversion to Christ was rather dramatic, so his new life in Christ was very different from the lifestyle he left behind. His knowledge of the Bible surpassed mine, and he was always eager to grapple with the harder or more philosophical questions about life and truth. We spent many hours discussing these weightier things about life and God.

One of the painful lessons I came to learn is that biblical knowledge and spiritual experience are not the same as emotional health or proven character. I don't say this as an accusation but as a descriptive. This was the truth about both of us. We were spiritually eager and hungry but probably thought more highly of ourselves and our spiritual strength and maturity than we ought. It's easy to talk about these things—it's another thing to live them out.

On my part, spiritual intimacy became intertwined with emotional intimacy, and spiritual and emotional intimacy, at least for women, makes you vulnerable to and desirous of physical intimacy. After all, this is how God designed us. I don't think I desired intimacy for intimacy's sake, but I think it was the longing for belonging and for covenant companionship. So, in keeping with God's design for the human heart, if we don't make choices to guard and protect our heart, then it will be violated and marred. Given my emotional insecurities at that time, which I was probably only somewhat aware of, I'm not sure I was even capable of guarding my heart.

When the deceiver of our souls can't get in the front door, he will look for a back door. In my case, this deception came in the form of a philosophical discussion with my boyfriend about what constitutes marriage before God. Could we be righteously married before God now (so that we could have sex) and then get legally married when the time was right? That when- the-time-is-right discussion always involves identifying things like money, education, maturity, stability etc., but I think it was the fear of commitment and responsibility that made us want to take a seemingly easier path to getting our intimacy needs met.

I knew something wasn't right about that line of reasoning on marriage, but I didn't have a good rebuttal, and, by this time, I was too emotionally invested in the relationship to risk a painful breakup. The leaven of this thinking, coupled with not seeking outside counsel or accountability (which was certainly available), led to the inevitable outcome of a sexual union. This is how a girl with strong convictions against sex outside of marriage gives into the pressure to have sex outside marriage. You see, I discovered that a theoretical covenant without an actual covenant is no covenant at all.

Once the door to deception is opened, it's easier to open the next one that comes along. About a year later, after we had left school and were trying to figure out our next steps, I found out I was pregnant. I was back in my hometown when I decided to get a pregnancy test. It was a snowy winter day. The roads were treacherous, but my need to know my possible plight felt greater than the risky road conditions. I dropped off my urine sample at the doctor's office and then tried to find an errand to engage myself in while I waited. By the time I went back to get the results, I was definitely anxious. As I approached the nurse's desk, I'm sure I looked pitiful and could've crumbled if anyone looked at me wrong. But I was determined to keep my composure. The nurse asked for my last name. Minutes later, she returned and held a card to my face that said *positive*. She then looked at me and with a curt tone asked, "What do you want to do?" At this point, I was so gripped with shock I don't know what I said, but I'm sure I mumbled something. My next impulse was to get out of there as fast as possible.

Reality got harsher with each interaction I had from there. I knew I had to tell my parents. It's not that I feared telling them, but I was ashamed, embarrassed, and didn't want to bring this kind of disappointment into our family. My first call, however, was to my boyfriend, who lived several states away. I thought I would first arm myself with some positive affirmation from him before talking to my parents. Even though I knew this was not what my boyfriend and I wanted right now, I still expected his response to be reassuring and that he would say, "Let's just go ahead and get married now." But that was not the response I got. His first response was anger and a distancing himself from me and this newly revealed fact. This was very shocking and hurtful, but I told myself it was just his initial reaction.

After several additional phone conversations with my boyfriend, another philosophical discussion came to the forefront. He said if I had an abortion, at least we would know that the baby would immediately be with Jesus.

What? Did I hear that right? Once again, I knew something wasn't right about that line of reasoning, but I didn't have a good rebuttal, and by this point, my fear of being abandoned was even more terrifying. The ultimate question that got thrown into my court was "Well, what are *you* going do?" How could I be hearing this? All the "*we*" statements I used to hear now became *you* statements. The only assurances I heard about the future were that if I had the abortion now, that would give us time to get better prepared for marriage someday after we were finished with school and had good jobs.

These interactions with my boyfriend were devastating, but at least I knew he wasn't the only support person in my life. When I first told my mother I was pregnant, she had already somehow sensed it. Only she and my sister were home when I told them. I'm so thankful that my family home was a safe place to be honest, to cry, and to fail. I knew I was loved and accepted despite my failures, but we still had a crisis to walk through.

Shame has a subtle way of creeping in and taking over right from the start if you don't take your thoughts captive and immediately look to Jesus. I remember my mother going to the yellow pages of the phone book. The next thing I knew, she was pointing to an abortion listing in Pittsburgh. I could see the fear and shame come over her as she whispered the word *abortion*.

I don't think my mother and I had ever had a talk about abortion. It was probably because it seemed irrelevant to us and our family. In the 70s and now early 80s, the only people talking about abortion were hard-core feminists, and they all seemed like hippies of the 60s to me. It's not like I ever heard a pastor talk about it or do a teaching on it. In fact, the only reason I had ever done any reading on it myself was because Francis Schaeffer and C. Everett Koop had just released a book and lecture series called *Whatever Happened to the Human Race,* and, ironically but providentially, my boyfriend and I went to hear them speak one night about a year before we would be confronted with the issue ourselves. It's funny how philosophical discussions can stimulate conviction but remain non-threatening if they remain academic.

It totally took me off guard that my mom was also suggesting abortion. I was quickly feeling outnumbered even though only a couple people knew. But the two people that did know were probably the two that carried the most influence in my heart. My sister, to her credit, was the only person who cautiously but with conviction said she thought I shouldn't have an abortion, but we quickly shut her down. I will always honor my sister for her courageous conviction.

My dad was out of town at the time, so he heard second hand through my mom when he got home. My dad and I never directly talked about it. I felt too ashamed and awkward, and I think he didn't know how to talk to me or what his role should be. From my parents' perspective, an abortion would protect me from the consequences of my already bad choices and my future would turn out better if this mistake could just go away. Like my boyfriend, they hoped that abortion would be the lesser of two evils. Once again, I was confronted with the power that my insecurities, my shame, and my pride held over me. I was letting these pressures and fears snuff out my convictions and courage. So once again, I violated my heart and my conscience, but this time I was conceding to an abortion.

On a cold January day in 1981, my father and mother drove me to the big city of Pittsburgh, Pennsylvania to have an abortion. We got lost once along the way, which I'm sure was an opportunity to see that we had indeed lost our way, but, eventually, we found our destination in the top floor of a big high rise in downtown Pittsburgh. I was completely naïve about what I was getting into, and I had no knowledge of what was going to happen to me that day. Even the name of the place was innocuous and sounded like a doctor's office.

The first thing I noticed when I walked in the waiting room was that it was filled with several men who all seemed to be smoking, watching TV, or aimlessly pacing. I didn't understand why they were there. I didn't realize that this was only an abortion clinic and that all those people in the waiting room were waiting on someone like me.

The first stop on this multi-phased event was the front desk, where you handed over your money. They got that out of the way first. Then they asked for my urine sample and gave me some papers to fill out. I was then put in a room with several other young ladies like myself. This was the first time I began to realize what was happening. We were all there for the same purpose and procedure. The thing I remember about this step was they were now going to educate us about what was about to happen. I recall that they showed an anatomical model of sorts, but it had nothing discernable in the uterus. There was never any mention of a developing baby, and they assured us that this procedure was going to be quick and mostly painless. If we did have pain, it would resemble menstrual cramps.

The other thing I remember is that they were very passionate and emphatic about their subsequent birth control presentation. They tried to convince us how important it was that we took with us these birth control devices or pills. The implication was that if we didn't, then not only would that be irresponsible, but we would find ourselves right back here in no time. I felt disdain toward them for wanting to shove their birth control down my throat. Besides, it represented another form of personal hypocrisy if I conspired.

The next step was to give us a few minutes to speak individually with someone I presume was a social worker. The only thing I remember about that interaction was that she asked me if this was my decision. I said yes and that no one was forcing me to do this but that I didn't think I would feel good about it afterward. She hesitated a few seconds and then asked me if I had any questions. I wondered if she was there to pick up on my ambivalent cues or if she was there to make sure the question was asked. It's not that I would have opened up to her anyway, but her role felt more like legal due diligence than care about my well-being.

Next was the final waiting room before you went in for your procedure. They put all of us young women in the same room once again as we waited for our names to be called out one by one. By this time, some of these women started to chat with one another. Some were nervously talking nonstop, some were trying to keep things light and superficial. One girl, who was quite vocal, shared that she was from a local Christian college. I remember wishing she would keep quiet because it was only adding to *our* bad witness. Others like me were waiting silently, not saying a word, and trying to detach from what was going on around me and inside of me. I thought about how far I had fallen from enjoying my new friendships at school, from all the things I was learning about the Bible and about God, and from the fun and adventure of my days at my Christian college to finding myself in a waiting room waiting to have my baby killed. How did this happen, and how could this be me? I was one of the last to have the procedure that day. Looking back, I had a lot of time to think and to watch what was going on around me and to change my mind and walk out, but I didn't.

This whole day weighed heavy on the hearts of my mom and dad as well. I think they were trying not to let their ambivalence show, thinking it would be better for all of us. They spent the whole day in the waiting room and overheard many things. My mom particularly felt compassion for one lady who shared some awful circumstances that surrounded the young woman she had accompanied to the clinic that day. My mom's heart also went out to another young man who was there with his girlfriend. He begged the clinic workers to allow him to go in with his girlfriend, but they wouldn't let him. I think my mom identified with his sense of helplessness and desperation.

As she shared these instances with me and how it broke her heart for those people, we talked about how one of the deceptions surrounding abortion is you hope it will be a solution to awful, seemingly impossible circumstances. That's why so many people think it's the lesser of two evils, but I assure you it's not. It's just evil, and it's a death that begets more death, in one way or another. In more recent conversations, my mom shared with me how she was fighting her own spiritual battle that day. The enemy, in turn, used it against her for years as a weapon of torment. She shared that at one point during that day, she went to the restroom. She was the only one in there, but she had a real encounter with the Lord. She said the Lord revealed Himself so clearly that day. She said it was as if she could see His arms being stretched out toward her—He was compassionately imploring her to just ask Him for help. My mom's biggest regret and heartache has been that she didn't yield to His invitation.

Later, when she and my Dad took a lunch break, she thought about writing me a note and having them send it in to me. It would say, "Let's just leave this place." But by the time they got back to the clinic, she saw that I was gone from that initial room and thought it was too late, so she didn't pursue it further. I can testify that the whole set up between the waiting room and what goes on behind those closed doors is very intimidating and seemingly off limits.

We both shed tears as we pondered how differently that day could have ended. Oh, how I wished I would've gotten that note, and oh, how I wished I would have had the courage to just walk out. How I wished I could have had eyes to see Jesus' arms extended toward me. He is faithful to show us a way of escape if we have eyes to see and ears to hear.

The next stop was the abortion procedure room. I remember it as cold. The doctor only said a few words to me, but I didn't want to talk to him anyway. The nurse was kind. This was a suction aspiration abortion. I'm sure they told us at least the basics about this procedure, but in no way was I prepared for the physical pain and the pressure I would feel. I believe they gave me a shot of Novocain, but I can't imagine what it would've been like without it. I've come to understand since then that the vacuum suction of those machines is around 29 times stronger than a household vacuum cleaner. It felt like my whole insides were being sucked out. It was very painful, and the whole experience was degrading—but I knew the trauma to my womb and what was being sucked out of it was far more grave than what I was experiencing physically.

These procedure rooms are death chambers indeed. I know many people who work in the abortion industry think they're helping women. The only way I can imagine they can continue to see what they see, hear what they hear, and do what they do day in and day out is they find a way to emotionally and spiritually quarantine their soul. The images they see, the screams they hear, and the tears that fall must be recorded on the hard drives of their souls, and you can only keep those internal accusing voices at bay for so long.

When you shed innocent blood, those stains do not wash off your hands with soap and water. Working in that industry and carrying that level of moral guilt (I'm not talking about guilt feelings, because whether you feel guilty or not does not determine if you are morally guilty) must be a little like the Hotel California: you can check out, but you can never leave. You can never escape the sin of bloodguilt that weighs on your soul. Unless you repent and cry out to the only One who can rescue your soul and cleanse your hands, your mind, and your heart from all unrighteousness.

The last stop of the day was the recovery room. If women were allowed to see the recovery room of an abortion clinic first, I'll bet most of them would turn around and walk out the front door. Here is your last view of the women you spent your abortion day with. No one was chatting, laughing, or making small talk anymore. Everyone was lying on cots, moaning, bleeding, crying, and trying to comprehend what had just happened to them.

The clinic has a protocol to complete before you get discharged. One of those was a nurse checking to see how heavily you were bleeding. I vaguely remember that after I was checked, I was given some follow-up instructions, a prescription for antibiotics, and oh yes, "Don't forget your birth control."

The most disturbing thing I remember from those last few minutes before they let us go was a final *pep talk* a nurse gave. She said, "Ladies, I know this has been a difficult day, but we need to be thankful that we live in a country where we have this freedom." If I hadn't been nauseated up to this point, I was now. Those words felt to me like Satan's mockery. It was as if he was putting his signature lie on the day, and not only did he win the day but he also handed everyone a lollipop for cooperating so well. I suspect his strategy was this: if he could make this day about freedom, then maybe we would feel as if we were part of a grand, noble cause. Then maybe we would keep silent about how we really felt. Many things that day were strange and confusing for me, but the one thing that was crystal clear was that what I had just participated in had nothing to do with freedom.

Next was the long ride home. At this point, what was there to talk about? It was a long day; we were all tired and,

I suppose, numb. I slept some. I also remember asking God to forgive me.

That night, I talked with my boyfriend on the phone. He was very sympathetic and comforting. We talked a bit about the future and getting married "when the time was right." These words of assurance were like the down payment on the hope for why I had the abortion in the first place. But you can't hang your hope on words, can you?

Every day over the next months seemed like one more day of distance from *that day*. We never acknowledged it, but I know we all wanted as much distance from it as possible.

Abortion is a trauma, and it's a trauma on every level physically, emotionally, spiritually, and relationally. But the strange thing is you're not sure you want to label it a trauma because then you would have to acknowledge that indeed it was a trauma. Your next preoccupation becomes bracing yourself for the fall-out. So while you're still trying to process what happened to you, you take a few steps forward, find normal again, and hope that maybe it wasn't an atomic bomb that went off in your soul.

I can identify a couple of dynamics that were going on in me in those first days and weeks. First, I believe I was experiencing the grace of God. He was holding my heart together probably like a triage intervention. The patient (me) is in shock so I wasn't really aware of my own condition, but the doctor knows full well what's going on. Secondly, I was especially sensitive to how my mother was processing all that had happened. I could sense a big weight on her, so I was trying to appear okay for her sake, and she was trying to appear okay for my sake.

About a month later, my fragile yet somewhat stable internal world came crashing down. I heard these words over the phone. "You know Karen, I think we made a big mistake. I've asked God to forgive us, and I think the best thing would be for us to move on and go our separate ways."

So there it was—my worst nightmare. The thing I was holding my breath about but trying to believe for the best actually happened. The very person and purpose for which I had the abortion in the first place was also gone, aborted right out of my life.

2

The Fallout and the Rebuilding

MY BOYFRIEND BREAKING UP with me was the first post-abortion earthquake I had to endure. Over the years, I experienced even more tremors and aftershocks. Earthquakes have a way of shattering your denial. But even from my vantage point today (decades later), I can say with full conviction "Praise God" for His merciful earthquakes. He could have left me in my self-made la la land where I thought denying the truth in my heart was somehow a safe place. A life that's not built on God's will and His truth is not a place of freedom, but a place that always needs to be managed. You can never fully rest in God when you're always bargaining with God. Sometimes He must let our idols topple before we will see them for what they are.

The breakup with my boyfriend also became a secondary earthquake for my mom. She also had hoped this was going to work out in the end and that somehow the abortion would have served a redemptive purpose in my relationship. But my pain only intensified her pain, guilt, and regret. One day shortly after my breakup, my mom came to me in tears, so sorry for the pain she felt she had caused by encouraging my abortion. I was not holding it against my mom or my dad—or my boyfriend for that matter—because I knew it was ultimately my choice. However, it was comforting that we could at least acknowledge our pain and regret together. Another thing we talked about recently is how different her perspective became as she got older. She now realizes that our family (she and my dad) was still young enough and that we could have all helped raise another child. Fear of what seems insurmountable will always blind us to the God of the impossible.

Within a couple of months, my need to tell someone or confess to someone about my abortion was increasing. I didn't have peace in trying to keep it all to myself or to handle it on my own. I was sad, hopeless, and full of shame. I wanted to share with someone, but I didn't know who or how. I was also reluctant because I knew my parents wanted to keep this as private as possible. Somehow I knew if I didn't bring at least my part and my sin into the light, this whole thing would fast become a skeleton in the family closet. The enemy loves family closets full of skeletons because, although these family secrets might save face for a season, they will also unleash a generational curse on the family line. I didn't understand all that back then, but I clearly understand it now.

During that time, the Holy Spirit was simply urging me to obey the word of God. James 5:16 says, "Therefore, confess your sins to one another and pray for one another, that you may be healed." In this verse lies a monumental truth and promise. The way to healing is to first confess our sins and then to pray for one another.

There was a lady from my church that I felt I could trust with my secret. I asked her if we could meet to talk (as scared as I was). We went for a long walk in the woods that day, and my story came tumbling out. I cried, she cried, and I think Jesus was crying, too. I will be eternally grateful for this lady and her love for me. I know she said some profound things that day, but what I mostly remember was her love, grace, and acceptance.

From this simple walk and my confession and her prayers for me, God honored my obedience to His Word—my healing had begun. I felt I could breathe again. As we finished up she said, "Karen, I feel like the Lord wants me to say to you that someday He's going to raise you up and you're going to minister to other women who've had abortions." I'm sure I had a stunned look on my face. I heard it with my ears, but I did not know how to begin to grasp it, but for that day I believe the Lord was just asking me to let this seed be planted in my heart.

Over the next four years, the Lord did a steady but intermittent work in my heart regarding my abortion. I believe He was doing a layer-by-layer approach to my healing and restoration.

Sometimes it looked like a private work just between Him and me. I would read a book or write out my thoughts and prayers in my journal. One time He gave me a poem. But other times, He wanted people to come alongside me in the journey. This was a much riskier feeling, but I came to understand it was absolutely necessary. In fact, if I had never crossed that bridge, then nothing you read throughout this book would have ever come into existence—at least not through me.

His grace was restoring my confidence in His grace, or maybe it was that His grace was being redefined in me, and I started to really understand what His unmerited favor meant. I had enough faith in God's grace that I knew I hadn't forfeited my salvation and that I would get to heaven someday, but the thought of meeting my children was a scary thought. What would I say? What would they say? I knew the Lord would cover that too, but it still caused me anxiety.

My main spiritual struggle in those first four years was not that I forfeited God's love or heaven but that I probably forfeited His good plan for me here on earth. I spent a lot of those years in different kinds of torment. For example, not a day went by when I did not think about the abortion. It haunted me. I could not say the word *abortion*. I would avoid it or any discussion of it like the plague. On the inside, I hated abortion, and I knew it meant death on every front. But on the outside, I was gaged and bound. I also became a target for the enemy's blackmail. If I thought about talking about it more openly, he threatened me with a lie (like I would bring more pain and shame on my family), so I stayed gagged and silent. Part of me thought I would just stay in the background of life and be a good church lady and not cause any trouble.

But guess what? God made this girl to roar! That's right! This mostly introverted girl from rural Pennsylvania who has always seen herself as an unlikely candidate for anything too risky is one God designed to pierce the darkness of the enemy's camp with the Holy Roar of His mercy, His grace, and His power to heal, deliver, and set the captives free! Hallelujah!

More to Go

Much to my surprise, during this time the Lord opened some opportunities for me to be involved in a ministry. I worked as a camp counselor for a couple of summers. He started to build up my confidence again that He could use me even while I was still an outpatient in His hospital. I led kids to Christ, I did Bible study with them, and I again enjoyed fellowship with other Christian peers.

I've learned over the years that the Lord will build you up as preparation for the next difficult reality check. During this time of being entrusted with ministry, I had two encounters that were necessary but terrifying to go through. First, I met a guy who expressed interest in getting to know me better. He also was one of the camp counselors and seemed bold in his faith and convictions. Great, I thought, I like that in a man. I think he had a gift of evangelism because he shared his faith freely and openly. We were having a good discussion one evening, and I was tracking with him in whatever we were talking about. Then suddenly, he brought up the *A* word. He began to passionately speak about the pro-life outreach he was involved in on his campus. I don't even know what he said after a few minutes because I was just trying to manage my racing heart and my emotions that were about to manifest in tears. I was trying to figure out how to either change the subject or leave the room.

Clearly, my heart was not free, and it only took that trigger to set it racing. I don't think he picked up on anything that night, but eventually, my friendship and trust in him grew enough that I could share my story. Even then, I couldn't bring myself to say the word *abortion*. But God in his grace allowed him to figure it out, and he said, "Karen, you've had an abortion, haven't you?" I was both relieved and terrified, but it felt good to get it out in the open with him. He didn't judge me, he didn't lecture me, and he showed me grace, acceptance, and forgiveness. That's exactly what my heart needed from him.

The next encounter came about a month later. I was with this same guy, and we were visiting a couple in their home. I was having a good time and felt relaxed. A visitor came by unannounced to drop off some posters for an event. These posters were pictures of aborted babies. I had no time to brace myself or prepare my response, but once again I was not okay on the inside. I excused myself and went to the restroom. About 15 minutes later when I hadn't come out, the wife came to check on me. I didn't need to say much—they figured it out. I could tell they felt badly about what had just happened. It was too awkward to continue the evening, so we left.

Through these events, the Lord revealed that I still had quite a way to go before I would walk in freedom. In fact, I didn't even know what healing and freedom would look like, but I knew I had a long way to go.

It was only because I gave the Lord permission to do His healing work in His way and in His time that He could work a healing strategy all along the way. He was always faithful to build me up in His love and affirmation. Therefore, I could have confidence that He was for me and not against me. As my confidence grew, I could handle the hard but necessary confrontations that revealed the still-broken condition of my heart. When I had the confidence of His love, I could be assured He wasn't punishing me nor were those people judging me. They were loving instruments in the Lord's hands that helped me continue my journey of being sweetly broken.

Accelerated Change

The winds of change were blowing, and I was about to enter a new chapter. I moved to the Tidewater area of Virginia to finish college. As part of my program, I had to do an internship in a human services agency. A new crisis pregnancy center had just opened in Virginia Beach. I didn't know everything these centers were about, but I knew they were Christian, and I already had a heart connection with the name. I set up an appointment with the director. I didn't know I wasn't going to permanently walk out of those doors until seven years later. The Lord was about to raise the stakes and put me on a fast track—I just had to keep my eyes on Him and follow His lead.

God will bring certain people into your life at strategic times that change the game for you. Vicki Gero was one of those people for me. Only God knows how vital it was that I had a Vicki for that time and season and how much she poured out and poured into me to prepare me for what God was calling me into. He used Vicki to teach me so many things. Some of it was taught, some of it was caught, but all of it was necessary. Vicki was the new director of the Crisis Pregnancy Center of Tidewater.

During my interview with her, I told her my story. She didn't flinch, and she encouraged me to take the next step of attending their volunteer training. I was eager to learn and eager to help other girls who were facing the same things I did. The training seminar was another milestone challenge for me. For the first time, I got a clear and in-depth understanding of what actually happens in an abortion procedure. For the first time, I heard about the physical and emotional risks. The veil was being lifted from the lies and half-truths

I was told at the abortion clinic. Each night of the training was another night of revelation for me. Vicki would ask me how I was doing with the information, and then she would pray for me and for each of my fears and my questions.

Through this training, I clearly saw the stages of fetal development in the womb—how beautiful and how fearfully and wonderfully made we are by an awesome Creator. I needed prayer as I processed those realities. I could see the stage of development that my babies would have been when they were aborted. Through this training I read and heard for the first time what the Bible taught about the sanctity and value of human life and how God viewed it. How had I never understood these things and our churches weren't teaching these things? God was gently but soberly walking me through layers of revelation, repentance, grief, and healing.

The time came for me to see my first client. "Am I ready for this, Lord? I'm probably more scared of her than she is of me." Those first several clients that God entrusted to me were as perfect for me as I was for them. I led one to Christ, and another allowed me to share my abortion story and then changed her mind about having an abortion. Again, He was building up my confidence and letting me see that He can take what Satan meant for evil in my life and use it for good.

My first years in the pregnancy center were in the mid- to late 80s. The pregnancy-center movement was still in its developing stages, so materials and resources were limited. We all learned as we went. We did not have an abortion-healing program in place, so it became one of my jobs to develop one. There was a new Bible study out called *Women in Ramah,* which is now called *Forgiven and Set Free*. I asked some of our volunteers who were post-abortive, along with a few clients, if they would join me in this study. We launched our first post-abortion Bible study and support group. I had attended a training seminar on how to lead it, but I was only about one step ahead of my group. I was both a group member and the leader (I kind of cringe at that now, but God covered it beautifully). We all went on this healing journey together.

Through these studies, I saw a depth of pain in women I had never seen before, and I heard stories I could scarcely imagine. God was exposing me to depths of wounds and horror I didn't even know existed.

During my years in the pregnancy center movement, I was single. It's one thing to be single in your mid-20s—it's another thing to still be single as you enter your early 30s. Abortion affects almost every area of your life in one way or another. I was weary of being single. I recognized that God knew what He was doing, and He obviously thought there was still work left to do in me before He would bring me a husband, but it was becoming a painful struggle. I desired to get married and have children like the next girl, but my answer was always "Wait."

By this time, I had a host of volunteers at the center who loved me and who loved to mother me and were praying for a husband for me. I had a few relationships at that time I hoped would end in marriage, but they ended in more heartbreak. But those heartbreaks also revealed places in me that were not yet emotionally healthy, and I believe the Lord was sparing me from even more disappointment and heartbreak down the road.

Then at long last, the Lord sent my knight in shining armor. He had a few dings in his armor too, but for the next leg of the journey, God would use us in each other's lives to continue our mutual restoration. I married at thirty-four years old, and I became a new (and inexperienced) stepmom.

Everything changed for me once again. I was no longer just my own caretaker and my own provider. I was now caretaking for four more people. I also joined my husband in the consulting company he started to help pregnancy centers develop. I continued to be a trainer for a national affiliate of pregnancy centers, but, for the most part, I laid down my direct ministry involvement in the movement. This was a new season, and I was ready to care for my new family as well as start a family of my own.

A Shocking Diagnosis

We were four years into our marriage, and I still hadn't got pregnant. I was 38 by now and time was slipping by quickly. I made an appointment with my doctor to have an initial conversation about our infertility issues and asked my husband to come with me. I was not highly anxious about the appointment, but I did feel emotionally vulnerable. I figured I would probably cry, and if I did, I'd rather have my husband there than to cry in front of my doctor, who I didn't know.

The appointment went fine. Dr. Johnson asked me several questions to gain understanding about my ovulation, etc. I had expressed that, although I was open to certain treatments regarding infertility, there were also certain boundaries I was unwilling to cross. If the Lord was going to give me a baby, I didn't want to force a Hagar situation—I wanted to trust God for His way. Dr. Johnson suggested a simple drug protocol that could regulate my ovulation. He said to give it some thought and then get back to him in a week. That sounded reasonable to me, and I didn't think I needed to give it much thought, but another week would be fine.

We were just about to wrap up the appointment when, seemingly out of nowhere, I asked, "Dr. Johnson, do you think I should have a mammogram?" I had no idea why I asked that question, and I was even a little embarrassed that I had. He too looked a little shocked. He flipped through my chart to check my age and said, "Let's see you're 38. We usually don't suggest a baseline until you're 40. I don't think it's necessary, but if you want one, I can certainly arrange it." I was just about to say that I didn't know why I even asked the question and had no reason to think I need a mammogram, so I'll wait a couple years. But then I looked at my husband and asked him what he thought. He simply said, "Sure, why not have one? It couldn't hurt." The next thing I knew, I had an appointment for a mammogram.

"Mrs. Ellison, we need you to come back in for another test. We saw something suspicious on your mammogram." What? Did I hear that correctly? I've never gotten a call back from a routine test, ever. This must be a mistake, but they want to cover all the bases. They ran another test and found breast cancer. It was a tumor in the beginning stages, and it was near my chest wall, so I wouldn't have felt a lump until it was considerably larger.

This diagnosis required a detour in our lives we certainly weren't planning on. After more tests, more consultations, and much prayer, our treatment plan unfolded. I had a lumpectomy. The surgeon wasn't satisfied with the pathology report, so I had a partial mastectomy. This time he was satisfied enough with the outcome. Following these two surgeries, I had seven weeks of radiation treatment.

I share this story to bring attention to God's fingerprints. The only explanation I have for why I asked Dr. Johnson about a mammogram in the first place is because the Holy Spirit planted the thought in my mind and overcame my *reasoning objections* long enough that I spoke before I could stop myself. I'm so thankful for the Holy Spirit's intervention!

Only the Holy Spirit knew that if He did not bring it to light when He did, I could have had a much different and dangerous outcome. If I had started taking a fertility drug at that time, it could have accelerated the cancer growth. It's been 20+ years since my bout with cancer, and I continue to be cancer free. Praise God!

I have no way of proving, nor do I have a need to prove, what I'm going to say next. I believe the same Holy Spirit who led me through the labyrinth I described above gave me revelation concerning my cancer. I believe the cancer was directly connected to my abortion. It didn't manifest until 16 years later, but I certainly wasn't thinking about the risk of breast cancer the day I went in for my abortion.

I want to make one more point about my breast cancer trial that I believe is central to the purpose of this book. Had I not received ongoing healing regarding my abortion, I could have interpreted my cancer battle totally different from how I did interpret it. If I had still been walking in guilt, shame, and self-imposed condemnation, then breast cancer would have seemed like the retribution I deserved. I would've viewed God as out to get me.

But that interpretation couldn't be further from the truth. I know now, and I knew then, that God loves me and He is for me. He is forgiving and merciful, and He rescued me from a destruction the enemy wanted to use to not only snatch my life but to also disillusion many other people who would have benefited from my story.

For more information on the abortion/breast cancer link, visit the Breast Cancer Prevention Institute at www.bcpinstitute.org
1

We are still living in the day of God's amazing grace and mercy. He is tarrying to give the people of this world every possible opportunity to hear His voice, recognize His warnings, and receive His forgiveness and love. Often, it's the mercy of God that allows the consequences of our sin to manifest so we will come running back to Him.

In my case, all the times He made me confront hard truths that I didn't want to face was His mercy that broke through the deception of my denial. And the trial of my breast cancer and the laying down of my ability to bear natural children (which I will describe next) were not God's wrath or condemning judgment as a result of my sin but were consequences of my sinful choices and were motivated by His unfathomable, everlasting, unconditional, can't-hide-from-it love and grace for me. Whatever consequences anyone in Christ might face, it's not the result of His wrath. His wrath has been satisfied. It may be a consequence that will lead us to His mercy and convince us of His love.

It needs to be stated, however, that if you are not a Christ follower and your name is not written in the Lamb's book of life and your sins are not covered by the blood of Jesus Christ, then you will not escape the wrath of God or the eternal condemnation and punishment for your sins, including the sin of abortion. I pray that you will persevere through this book and allow God to reveal Himself and His love to you. At the end of the next chapter, there is a prayer of salvation that you can pray to secure your identity as a child of God and the forgiveness of your sins. He loves you more than you can imagine, and He is inviting you home.

Moving to Tennessee

My family moved from Vista, California, to Knoxville, Tennessee, at the end of 1998. For my husband Arthur, this was moving back home to where he grew up. I loved Knoxville and was happy to start a new chapter in our lives.

Before we left California, I had a consultation with my doctors about resuming fertility options. They gave me a green light but suggested I get settled from this move because moving your whole life across the country is stressful.

It took about two years for us to get totally settled and in the groove of our new beginning. At the end of our first year in Knoxville, when I prayed about seeking out a fertility specialist, I never felt a peace in my spirit. It's not that I heard God say no—it was more like the Lord wasn't ready to address it yet. I was okay with that, so I just kept moving forward. By the end of the second year, I needed a resolution to my unanswered prayers regarding bearing children. My prayer went something like this: "Lord, You know we've walked through a lot of things together, and You know I trust you. You know my heart's desire is to have a baby, but I do not want to be desperate for a baby, I want to be desperate for You and what You have for me. If the answer is no, then I think I can hear it now, but I need you to bring resolution to this one way or another. Oh, and, Jesus, whatever it is, please be gentle."

Two major developments emerged in our lives at this point. My husband and I were starting another ministry that was initially birthed within the pregnancy center movement. It was a paradigm shift for some. It was a call to begin to lead from a new place of being in God's presence in intentional ways and seeking His face through times of worship and intercession. Out of these times, worshiping Him would become the main objective and receiving direction would be secondary. This was a new and exciting adventure and had the feel of revival fires beginning to burn within the movement. We named the ministry 2nd Question, which came from Joshua 5:14.

At that same time, I also started to volunteer at a local pregnancy center. I had met the director, Sharon Anderson, while we still lived in California, and now we were attending the same church in Knoxville. She had asked me if I would come and help get a post-abortion ministry started at her center. I wasn't sure I was ready to jump back into all of that, but I told her I would pray about it. I sensed the Lord telling me yes, so I started to put together a Bible study/support group, which was the only thing I knew how do to. We attempted two different groups, and although the Lord is always faithful to show up and touch people in amazing ways, our attempts didn't seem to gel. It was like a perfect storm that He used to clear the deck and help me think in a new way.

I was just about to tell Sharon I didn't think I could continue doing these groups when the Lord broke into my thinking and gave me another approach—a retreat. He said to start by writing down all the areas that I knew were foundational to healing the wounds of abortion and that He would teach me step-by-step how to expand them and implement them. I called Sharon and told her I had a wild idea, and I asked her if she would trust me to run an experiment. In 2001, I began what I call a primitive attempt at a post-abortion healing retreat. I thank the Lord for the three different directors I worked under over a period of seven years who gave me much grace and latitude as Deeper Still was being knit together.

Closure and New Beginnings

In May 2001, God met me in such a profound way to bring my heart the much-needed answer about bearing children, for which I had been waiting for years now. We were in the middle of a 2nd Question board meeting in Lancaster, Pennsylvania. My husband Arthur was chairing the meeting, and he was at the head of the conference table. I was sitting at the other end of the table. He led us into a time of quiet listening and waiting on the Holy Spirit to see if He wanted to speak to us. This was not an unusual request because this was part of the new paradigm of listening that the Lord was teaching us.

I had nothing particular on my mind other than musing over some things we had discussed earlier. So once again I was "minding my own business" as I quieted myself before the Lord, like everyone else in the room. After about a minute, I began to have this strange sensation that felt like it was deep in my gut. Then my heart started pounding. I had no idea what was happening, but I knew it was the Holy Spirit hovering over me and stirring up something inside me. I wasn't afraid, but I felt vulnerable. The sensation in my gut seemed to rise upward, and then I started crying. It felt like deep sobs of grief. I still didn't know what it was about, but I kept yielding to it, believing it was the Holy Spirit doing a work.

By this time, everyone in the room had figured out that something was going on with me. They began praying softly to themselves. My friend Luann, who was sitting next to me, put her hand on my back and started praying. She told me later that she felt my heart beating through my back.

After a few minutes, I began to understand what was going on. I felt like the Lord was saying, "Karen, this is your day, this is the day you've been waiting for. This is the day, and I'm asking if you will lay down on my altar your hope to bear a child. You are among friends you love and trust, and I'm giving you an opportunity to grieve openly among friends as a witness to the work I'm completing this day."

As these thoughts flooded into my mind, I felt my heart yielding as I said, "Yes, Lord, I will lay it down. But, Lord, I just have one fear. If I lay this down, will I lose my mother's heart? You've restored so much about my mother's heart, because part of it was aborted that day too. Do you really want me to give that up too?" Then I felt His affirmation as He said, "No. It's because of your mother's heart and its capacity that I'm asking you to lay down an earthly fulfillment of that desire. If you will lay the natural way down, I will place in your arms a supernatural blessing that will restore the hearts of many mothers, and you will be released and empowered to mother many." I began to share that as best I could with everyone in the room. They prayed for me, and my heart was comforted.

At one point during that experience, I felt hands on my shoulders. When I looked back, I saw that it was my husband Arthur and he was praying for me. Later, he shared with us his experience. He said just before I started crying, he had felt a crushing pain in his chest. He thought he might be having a heart attack and almost asked someone to call an ambulance, but he hesitated for a few minutes, thinking it might be spiritual. Then as I began to share, he came over and put his hands on me, and when he did, the Lord told him that He was allowing him to feel his wife's pain—that her heart was breaking, but He was doing a work. These words were so comforting to me because I didn't just want this to be my story—I wanted it to be our story.

Pregnant with Deeper Still

I didn't immediately understand that it was Deeper Still that God was fashioning in me and that He was giving it to me to raise and nurture and release to the world, but as time went on, that became more and more clear to me. The time and sacrifice it has taken to grow Deeper Still has been way more than I imagined. If I were raising another child, I could not have given myself as fully to parenting or as fully to this ministry as both would need. It's not that I no longer grieve the loss of bearing natural children, but I've never gotten stuck in it, and I've never despised my earthly losses. The Lord has given me so many spiritual daughters and sons that my quiver is overflowing. I am a blessed woman, and I am full of joy!

If it weren't for the Lord's faithfulness and intervention in my life, I could have become embittered over some of the trials that I've walked through in later years. If my heart and mind had not been healed, I could still be interpreting some of my life experiences as God's judgment and punishment—void of His love. The Bible says that the thief (Satan) comes only to steal, kill, and destroy (John 10:10). Without God's intervention and our saying yes to His intervention, our lives would look like an old ravaged and plundered house.

But when we let the Savior rescue us, He will take every loss and make it a gain. Some of the gain may not be fully realized until heaven, but we at least get the down payment while here on earth. The enemy has lost so much more on me than he has ever gained, and I can truly say that Proverbs 31:25 has been manifested in my life: "Strength and dignity are her clothing, and she smiles at the future."

A Charge for All of Us

My story is the backdrop for this book, but this book is written for you. This book is intended to be both informational and experiential. In the chapters ahead, I will describe and define the abortion-wounded heart. I will also share more of my journey. I've included several testimonies of people who have found healing and lasting freedom as they have allowed the Savior to take them on a journey that resulted in receiving beauty for ashes. If you have an abortion-wounded heart, it matters to God. Reading this book may be the lifeline you have been looking for, so grab on to it, and He will meet you and heal you layer by layer.

This book would not be complete without addressing the men—our brothers and the fathers of our children. Your heart matters. Your story matters. Your leadership matters.

I'm also including a charge to the Church. We are the Bride of Christ, and we have been commissioned to help the Bride make herself ready for His return (Revelation 19:7). This Bride is broken, anemic, and feels unworthy to worship her Bridegroom in spirit and truth. Let's find ways to stand in the gap for her restoration so she is ready for that great day.

My prayer is that if you find yourself in the pages of this book, you will grab on to the hope available for you and will not stay stuck, but instead will grab on to the hem of His garment and beg Him for healing. If you're seeking to be better equipped to minister to the abortion-wounded, I thank you and commend you for expanding your tool belt. I believe God has treasures for you in this book.

As the days draw near for Christ's return, the pain and desperation people live with will become increasingly more difficult to stuff and deny. When everything that can be shaken will be shaken and the condition of men's hearts revealed, then fear will be rampant. But those who have ears to hear will be crying out for a Savior and a deliverer. Let us ready ourselves to address the coming flood.

Healing Exercise

Sharing You Story – if you have had an abortion or have participated in an abortion, the first step in starting your healing journey is to share your story with someone. If you keep your abortion secret and in the dark, you will never find healing or freedom. This is an area where Satan will try to blackmail you and convince you that bad things will happen if you reveal your secret. Just like mold in a basement, guilt, shame, and fear will thrive in the dark. But once it is exposed to sunlight, it begins to dry up. When hidden sins are brought into the light, the strongholds of fear, shame, and pride begin to lose their grip.

> But, if we walk in the light as He Himself is in the light, we have fellowship with one another, and the blood of Jesus His Son cleanses us from all

> sin…If we confess our sins, He is faithful and just to forgive us our sins and to cleanse us from all unrighteousness. (1 John 1:7–9)

> Therefore, confess your sins to one another, and pray for one another so that you may be healed. (James 5:16a)

> He who conceals his sins does not prosper, but whoever confesses and renounces them, finds mercy. (Proverbs 28:13)

Sharing your story with a trusted friend or spiritual mentor will also break the power of denial. When left to your own thoughts and perspective, you will continue to rationalize and justify your decisions even though you remain conflicted about it in your heart. Trying to keep sins hidden and managed is like trying to keep a volcano from erupting. The pressure will only increase over time. If you do not have a person in your life right now that you can trust, start asking God to send you one. He will be faithful to send you the right person at the right time.

I also want to assure you that God is for you. He wants to set you free more than you can imagine. He is compassionate and full of mercy. He will not expose you, but He will cover you.

> He will cover you with His pinions, and under His wings you will find refuge; His faithfulness is a shield and buckler. (Psalm 91:4)

> The Lord is near to the brokenhearted, and saves those who are crushed in spirit.
> (Psalm 34:18)

The best way to share your story is to write it out. Take time to put your story into words. Ask God to help you remember important details. How you experienced your abortion(s) and the circumstances around it is as important as the facts of your story. Don't just write the facts but share how your abortion affected your heart. Once you've written it out and are ready to share with someone, you will find it easier to share if you can read out loud.

Here are a few questions that can help bring your story into focus.

- What were the circumstances surrounding that time in your life?
- What caused you to make the decision to have an abortion?
- What memories do you have about the abortion(s) itself?
- How did your life and who you are change after the abortion(s)?
- What areas do you know you still need a healing touch?
- What would freedom look like for you?

3

The Abortion-Wounded Heart

THE MOST INNOCENT VICTIM of abortion is the baby whose life has been snatched away. The hope of all involved is that this incident, this mistake, would soon be forgotten and that a new beginning would spring forth. Time reveals however, it's never that simple and never that final.

The effects of abortion cannot be fully calculated on the front end. A woman may have read a list of possible side effects from abortion, or she may have even heard the testimony of someone living with an abortion-wounded heart, but, still, the emotional impact is not convincing enough to dissuade her from her decision to move forward. You see, once she sets her mind toward rationalizing her way of escape, her first defense is to block her emotions.

She's counting on being able to handle whatever consequences come her way. Regrettably, the depth of damage caused by an abortion usually doesn't hit home until after it's too late.

The wounds from abortion can be described as systemic. By this, I mean the effects of abortion can be like a cancer in your core identity. It gradually and even silently runs through the organs and blood system of your soul and then, eventually, it begins to manifest on many levels.

There have been many things written on Post-Abortion Stress Syndrome (PASS) and many psychological and emotional symptoms can be identified as PASS. My focus, however, is going to be on what I've come to observe as common emotional, relational, and spiritual bondages that manifest to one degree or another in anyone with an abortion-wounded heart.

I'm going to walk you through a common scenario for many women who choose abortion, and then we'll look at what happens afterward as they begin to experience the fallout. I'm including testimonies from several women who have lived out these scenarios. Each of the testimonies is from people whom I've come to know because they have been participants in our Deeper Still retreats. For them to be able and willing to share their stories comes at a great price. But because they're now walking in freedom from their past choices, they're eager to share their stories if they would be a lifeline for others. For every painful account you will read in this book, there is a miraculous, redemptive new story being lived out.

Her Mindset

Let's first think through what happens when a woman is contemplating an abortion. What is her frame of mind, and what is her expectation? When a woman is abortion-vulnerable, it almost always means she's scared. But other forces are also driving her decision. Either she's under tremendous pressure from other people to abort, or her overwhelming circumstances cause her to conclude that she has no other choice. Or maybe she does not consider herself in crisis but, for her, having a baby would be too much of an inconvenience, so she wants an out.

Depending on her knowledge of pregnancy and abortion, she may or may not know what the abortion procedure entails, but even at this point, she's thinking the less she knows the better. So into the clinic she goes, with her defenses already up. When she enters the abortion clinic, her first stop is the front desk. There she will pay the fee for the service she's about to receive. The service she is paying for has many steps and concludes several hours later. The end result is that she will no longer be pregnant. Just to be clear, the service she is paying for is that when she leaves the clinic, she will not be pregnant.

If this is her first pregnancy and her first abortion, she's hoping that what the clinic workers assurances are true—that "it" is merely tissue at this stage and should not be considered a baby. So with cautious relief, she agrees to take the next step. In her mind, she tries to minimize what's about to be vacuumed out of her womb. If she is further along in her pregnancy, the procedure gets more complicated, risky, and more traumatic than a vacuum- aspiration abortion. Nonetheless, she's trying to think about it in the same way as when she had her gallbladder removed. It was a little painful, but once she recovered, life resumed and she never gave it another thought.

Susan shares:

> I flew to New York by myself. I didn't talk to a single person. I couldn't even look at anyone. I was so afraid that if I did, they would know why I was on that plane. I was met at the airport by a

> limo and driven to the abortion clinic. The waiting room was dimly lit with soft plush furniture, magazines all around, soft music playing—spa-like. My name was called, and I was led into a sparse, sterile, brightly lit room where I undressed and was strapped in the stirrups. Then I saw it—a huge, silver vacuum-cleaner-like canister. I wanted to scream, "God, help me! Somebody, please stop me!" That's the last thing I remember. When I woke up in the recovery room, the long 42 years of covering up and living with the fear of somebody finding out what I had done began.

She may not be able to give you a definition of denial, but denial is about to become her new best friend. At this point, she doesn't realize how much energy it's going to take to manage her denial. If she determines that denying her conscience, her emotions, and even her intellect is what it's going to take to live with her abortion decision, then that's what she'll do. Denial will become her new go-to companion for the rest of her life, if necessary.

Armed with denial, emotional detachment, and a determination to believe what the clinic workers told her, she moves forward. She's counting on the impact to be minimal. This assumption is a welcomed relief because, afterward, she has plans for the day. For my friend, Sharon, later that day she would fly to another state to be a bridesmaid in her best friend's wedding. Sometimes denial serves as a survival technique. A woman will rationalize that if it's a quick outpatient procedure and statistically her chances of hemorrhaging are minimal, it might help if she had something celebratory planned afterward. "Besides everyone is counting on me," she tells herself. "I'll be fine."

Abortion Marketing

Let's address the marketing strategy of the abortion industry. It's incredibility effective because it tells us exactly what we want to hear. They say the only real risk is physical complications, but supposedly that's only in rare cases. Beyond that, the only challenge is getting through hormonal adjustments.

But as it turns out, those hormonal adjustments can have quite a jarring effect on the female pregnant body. When the natural flow of pregnancy hormones is abruptly stopped, there are residual effects. Can you imagine that it might be a little alarming for a young woman after she's had an abortion and has been told that it was just a mass of tissue to discover a liquid substance seeping from her breasts, because her mammary ducts have already begun to produce milk? *How does mere "biological tissue" have the power to produce milk,* she briefly ponders? But then again, she assures herself, "We all know hormones can be complicated."

The marketing pitch goes something like this: *Pregnant? No worries! We can make it as if you were never pregnant in the first place. You have the power of choice, and we have your solution. The procedure is quick, it's basically painless, and it's not that expensive—that is, compared to having a baby, but oops ... that's right, it's not really a baby. And best of all, you're in, you're out, and no one needs to know. In fact, you can make your afternoon class if we get you started early enough.*

So there you have it—a safe and quick solution with minimal risk and no moral implications.

But wait! What's happening to me? Why can't I stop thinking about that abortion? It's been five years now—what's my problem?

She eventually discovers that her now-familiar companion, denial, only shields her from a deeper reality going on inside her soul. The procedure that was supposed to liberate her is now seizing her identity, and she's starting to feel like a victim of a much larger ruse. What she once dismissed as "no big deal" is now haunting her. With a pit in her stomach, she now realizes that the abortion was not just a surgical procedure to remove that "inconvenient tissue," but, in fact, it was a deep violation to her soul and body, and she's left empty, sad, angry, and with blood on her hands.

It's like an enemy has taken up squatting rights in her soul, and, with each passing year, it's claiming more and more acreage. At first, she could fight off the feelings of regret as a hasty decision of her youth. But now it's taking more and more energy to manage her internal demons. She finds herself working harder and harder to excel at something worthy. She's determined to be a better person to make up for those feelings of self-hatred and disgust that keep encroaching.

She used to only hear those accusing voices at night when she tried to sleep. She had to enlist the help of sleep aids to fight that battle for her. But now the accusations are finding her while she's at work, and they're especially loud when something bad happens—like when she got passed over for a promotion, when her car broke down on the highway, or when her boyfriend broke up with her. Most recently, she's been battling an autoimmune disease and was told she's too stressed out.

This has to be God punishing me. There . . . I finally said it out loud.

Secrecy

For the woman who's had an abortion, her life takes on the new and determined characteristic of secrecy. She finds a place in her soul where she can hide and bury the memory of her aborted child. She hopes that the corpse buried in the attic of her soul will not give off an odor, or that the skeleton in the closet of her memories will not make any noise. She discovers, however, that it takes a lot of energy to mask the stench in the attic and to keep the skeleton from rattling.

Marie shares:

> The bondage of secrecy is like being gagged, bound, thrown into the water, and always feeling as if you're drowning. I would ache inside and never feel whole. I had been living in this kind of secrecy for over 30 years. By this time, I had grandchildren whom I love dearly. My greatest fear was that if my children ever found out about my abortion, they would not let me see my grandchildren anymore.
>
> It wasn't until I finally allowed the Lord to free me from those shackles that my heart could begin to heal. I could then trust Him to exchange my life of secrecy for a new life of authenticity and truthfulness. The time came for me to tell my children. Each one was accepting, forgiving and thankful I shared my story. They never even considered withholding my grandchildren.

Kim shares:

> For the past 17 years, I gripped my secret tightly. I didn't want anyone to know that part of me. I lived by perfectionism—to look perfect on the outside is to cover up the inward mess, chaos, hurt, shame, and guilt. Since my retreat, I can acknowledge that my abortion isn't something that defines me. It isn't something I am held captive by. It is an event of my past that I am wholly forgiven for by my Heavenly Father, who loves and adores me.

Shame

After an abortion, shame becomes the new garment she wears. Shame will either make her shrink away, never to be heard from again, or it will make her exert a self-determination that says, "Shame is not going to conquer me," and she will try to cover it over with myriad things, such as anger, bravado, perfectionism, good deeds, or success. Shame also has a way of seizing her identity and can open the door to self-hatred.

Cultural or familial shame can also have real consequences for people. The fear of open ridicule will further motivate a woman to keep her abortion a secret. In the context of a family culture, her abortion can just be another family skeleton in the closet, and she now becomes obligated to continue the family secrets. If bringing her abortion out of the closet and into the light will bring about family shaming, community gossip, or church condemnation, she will conclude that it's better to keep it all in the dark, even though it will fester into a slow death for her soul.

Linda shares:

> This is how I felt inside: "Hello, my name is shame!" When I was 19, I met a boy. I never had a boyfriend before—I was naïve. I ended up pregnant. I didn't talk to my mom about it because she was grieving the loss of my dad. I just handled it—I just fixed it. I didn't tell my boyfriend, my girlfriends—I told no one! I looked in the yellow pages and figured out what to do. I got the cash, and I did it. I did it twice in the same year. I handled it, and I stuffed it! I had my abortions early on, so it was just tissue and not my babies, right? I tried to believe the lie. This began the cycle of condemning thoughts, feelings of dirty shame, depression, low self-esteem, and hopelessness.

Catrina shares:

> I never really knew what shame was, but boy, was I walking a life full of it. I was living a life full of shame.

Sheppard shares:

> As a result of my abortion, I felt intense shame that kept my head down and my mouth shut. I remember a Christian counselor telling me that when I first came to his office, and for weeks

after, I would sit with my head down, avoiding eye contact, unable to answer any of his questions or to share what was going on in my life. On the inside, I was beyond desperate and grasping for any bit of hope that life would be "normal" again, but shame kept me silent and afraid. It not only silenced my voice, it also robbed me of my identity.

I now know and receive that the Lord has called me by name, redeemed my life, and restored what the locust has eaten—all beginning with this weekend retreat where I was able to receive His mercy, grace, and unending love for me. The shame I had lived with for so long that it had become a part of me was demolished and is no more.

Grief and Regret

Whether it's acknowledged or not, the soul of a post-abortive woman knows there has been a deep loss. She clings to denial to protect herself from defining or pondering her loss. She knows there is no turning back from her decision, so she does her best to keep it hidden. But unacknowledged grief cannot stay down forever. There will be "triggers" along her path of life. When her guard is down, there is an opportunity for the truth to surface. If she's determined to "not break," these triggers will feel like landmines in her never-ending war within herself. But if she can yield to facing the truth and name her loss, then she's on the road to redemption.

Here are two poems written by Patricia. She had stuffed her abortion and never gave it a thought for years. She eventually experienced what she calls an awakening. These words came once she acknowledged her loss, her grief, and regret.

Patricia's first poem:

> Tiny seed, baby new, did mommy every cry for you? Hidden deep inside my womb, a sanctuary turned to tomb. Did you feel any pain that day – when suddenly your life was sucked away? I saw the jar – clear glass with red; no hands would ever cradle your head. How many were there in that liquid bed – In the clear, glass jar filled up with red?

Patricia's second poem:

> I walked down the hall and into that room; that room, for hundreds became a tomb. What was I thinking? Why didn't I run? I lay on the table—the murder begun. The sound of the suction, a motor that hummed—so soon it was over this life just begun. There were four in that room, doctor, nurse, mother, child—three walked away—one forced to stay, never to see the light of day!

Gagged and Silenced

She also notices a difference in her social interactions. She always considered herself savvy enough to engage in conversations that were potentially controversial. But now if abortion comes up in a conversation, her heart begins to race and her face flushes. In fact, she can't even say the word *abortion*. She finds a way to either change the subject or leave the room. She fears that if she doesn't leave the room, she may have a meltdown in front of everyone. Because if she did start talking about it, everyone would immediately see the big *A* she now wears on her forehead, and they would all know.

After an abortion, most women will shrink back from speaking out on issues regarding human life, because they have been gagged and silenced by the guilt and shame that hold them captive. When those shackles fall off, however, the captives get set free, and they begin to get their voice back. The women who have gone through our retreats can begin to encourage others to come out from the shadows and live. Some of the Deeper Still participants have gone on to become part of the ministry team or start Deeper Still chapters.

Kim shares:

> Prior to Deeper Still, I couldn't say the word abortion . . . I couldn't even type it.

Catrina shares:

> If you were to ask my opinion on the subject, I had none, because how could I? How could I stand before someone and tell her not to do it and that it would be a brief moment in time that would haunt you for a lifetime? After all, I did it, and I was a "good Christian," so who was I to tell someone the price to pay would be everything? But since my retreat and my healing, I no longer

> cringe when I hear the word abortion, nor do I shy away and act as if I have no opinion. I do have a voice now that I never had before.

Kay shares:

> As I began to come out of my pit and grow in my faith, I could talk about all kinds of ways God was working in my life. But I still couldn't say anything about my abortion. I still had too much shame and condemnation on me. I was so worried about other people judging me and rejecting me. The only people who knew about my abortion were my husband and my sister. I avoided the subject like the plague. After my retreat, however, all that changed. I not only got my voice back and was able to openly share about my abortion story, but God began to birth in my heart a vision for how I could help others find deliverance and healing from their abortion wounds.

Looking for Love

Although it may take years of managing the symptoms before the post-abortive woman dares to look behind that wall of denial, she comes to realize that she's exhausted and that she can't fix her own broken and hardened heart. She would prefer to never bring another person into her secret self-help approach, but her soul is never satisfied by her own efforts. She reluctantly acknowledges that her relationships lack the freedom of authenticity. The relationships that she had hoped would ease the pain and her feelings of hopelessness and her need for love never came through for her. No one could get to the deep places of her thirsty soul.

Heather shares:

> My first abortion was when I was 19 years old. I was on a path of self- destruction and was in such denial. I had also gone with two other girlfriends to get their abortions. After my abortion, I went emotionally numb to cope with the reality of what I did. I went out with a girlfriend that night and got drunk. I began coping with my pain by stuffing it with social drinking to the point of blacking out several nights a week. I felt haunted, and I felt that I deserved punishment for what I had done. My promiscuity only escalated, as did my drinking. I got pregnant again and had my daughter and tried to get my act together. I even managed to finish college and get my teaching credentials. I was still participating in self- destructive behaviors but kept my daughter from seeing it. I was drinking when out with friends, sleeping with strangers for attention and love, and, eventually, I had an affair. I was living two lives. One that looked professional on the outside and another that, on the inside, was lost, insecure, and full of self-hatred. Later, I got pregnant again with another boyfriend, and we also decided to have an abortion. This time I was put to sleep, thinking I wouldn't feel the pain of my baby being ripped out again. That night we both went out drinking to cope with our choice. We

> eventually got married, but our marriage was doomed from the beginning. We finally divorced.

Expected Retribution

The post-abortive woman also begins to admit that she has certain expectations about her life. Retribution is stalking her, and someday when she's unguarded and taking a few minutes to enjoy life, it will pounce on her and demand payment.

Tina shares:

> From the day I found out that I was pregnant with Gregory (my first child after my abortion), another fear that crept into my life and choked me was the fear that something horrible would happen to him and that it was my fault because God was punishing me for my abortion. I lived with a constant nagging torment that I didn't deserve him and I wasn't worthy to be his mom. I had this panic within my heart that something tragic would happen to him because I could never live up to being an adequate mother.

Ginger shares:

> Before I went on the retreat, I was driving down the interstate, crying and praying to God that if He was going to take this baby in my womb by miscarriage that I would understand because of my abortion. However, all I have felt since the

> retreat all I felt is His amazing unconditional love and peace. My God loves me and gave me a second and a third chance to be a mom. I am incredibly blessed.

My Choice That Took Others Hostage

Now that she's carried this burden for several years and can't seem to shake it, she finds it harder and harder to dismiss her abortion as an "unfortunate necessity" of her youth. Because what she thought would only amount to a blip in the road on the way to her future dreams has now become a monster swallowing up her identity. Her life and dreams have been hijacked by a force far more sinister and powerful than she ever imagined.

When she contemplated having the abortion, she gave herself a few minutes to ponder a worst-case scenario. She concluded that even if she were one of those rare exceptions that needed a little more time to get over it, she would take responsibility for her own choices and any collateral damage would be limited to just her. She didn't plan on telling anyone, so her secret could just live and die with her. She soon realized, however, that it would never be just about her.

Tina shares:

> I had not a single indication or clue what a hidden, spiritually dark, crippled life I was about to enter into. After leaving the abortion clinic, I remember being totally out of control as if something had entered and possessed me—outrageous behavior of screaming, beating on the

> car, hitting the father of the child. I was overcome with feeling so repulsed I could vomit my insides out. Anger took residence in my life. Even years later, my family had to live with my uncalled-for anger, my expectations of perfectionism, and my controlling behavior. These behaviors in themselves are difficult to live with, but some days I would seem to have it all together, so the roller-coaster ride gave us all whiplash!

Marriage

But she hopes a new relationship can mean a fresh start. She puts her heart out there again (or part of her heart) and starts over with a new man, new circumstances, and new dreams. After a while, she could even imagine herself marrying him. They talked about many things over the months but mostly focused on their future together. When it came to their past, neither one felt it was necessary to disclose too much, so right from the beginning, they established an informal don't ask, don't tell policy for their marriage. She thought she trusted the man she married, but why could she not bring herself to tell him about her abortion(s)?

Erin shares:

> It was difficult for me to get close to my husband. My trust had been broken so many times from others that I couldn't bridge that gap between me and my own husband. As a result, he never got my whole heart.

Linda shares:

In my first marriage, I did tell my husband about one of my abortions. It was just a mention. I didn't go into any detail, and he didn't ask. I felt as if I needed to be as honest as I could let myself be, for our marriage. When our marriage began to fall apart, I was terrified he would tell my family out of revenge. In my second marriage, I didn't tell him. My abortions were stuffed down deep, and I was just not going to go there!

From the time I had my abortions, shame, guilt, depression, and self-condemnation became a part of who I am. Stuffing my secret affected all my relationships, but it especially affected my marriages. Intimacy means transparency, acceptance, and closeness. My secret was an obstacle, and it was crippling me in ways I didn't even recognize at first. Anything that went wrong in our relationship, I would take the blame. I thought maybe if I dressed better, kept the home spotless, was more attentive, or I were just a better person, we would have a better marriage. I was broken, and I worked so hard at covering up my inner ugliness.

After years of trying to keep my past sins and brokenness hidden and irrelevant to my present life, I ended up leaving a trail of two broken marriages, lost custody of two of my children, and I faced another custody battle for my youngest daughter. I finally came to the end of myself. But thankfully, that's right where God met me. It was at that moment of feeling completely rejected by all the people I had loved that God spoke into my

> life and said that He loved me! That moment started my journey out of the pit and into hope, healing, and freedom from my abortion-wounded heart.

Recommended article: "Can Relationships Survive After Abortion?" | AfterAbortion.org] [2]

Mothering

A few years later when they start their family, things get even more complicated. She can't figure out why her relationship with her kids is so erratic, especially with her firstborn. She vacillates between doting over them and even being hyper-controlling of them (to keep them safe, of course), but at the same time, she realizes she actually functions better when she relates to them from a management perspective rather than from a mothering heart. In this scenario, the fruit of her womb does not feel like her reward (as the Bible teaches), but more like a test to pass.

She feels good about the responsibility of raising her children because it feels like a significant endeavor, and their accomplishments can also become her accomplishments. Their emotional needs and development, however, is another issue. Although it's hard to admit, she finds herself parenting from her head more than from her heart. Trying to help them process their emotional needs and conflicts can become another academic exercise or a teaching point. But when she recognizes that her children are operating in denial or avoidance over something emotionally painful, she realizes that for her to confront that weakness in them is hypocritical on her part. So her attempts to model lack conviction, integrity, and authority.

Paula shares:

> My boys were almost one year old when I had my abortion. After my abortion, I found it difficult to love and pour affection onto my boys. I didn't nurture them as a loving, doting mother would, and I didn't cuddle them much. I felt guilty for loving them after killing their sibling. I threw myself into my own pleasures and pastimes—anything that would keep me from thinking about what an awful mother I was. I felt guilty whenever I got a sitter to watch them, yet I couldn't bring myself to just stay home and be a mom. I didn't give a thought to how my neglect might affect them down the road.

Pam shares:

> I instinctively knew the baby I aborted at the age of 16 was a boy. I stuffed my abortion down and went on with life. I later married and had a daughter, but when I was 30, I got pregnant with another boy and life completely changed for me. Not only could I not believe what the ultrasound said but also an oppressive fear came over me. The lie I lived under was this—you killed your first son, and you don't deserve another. Therefore, God is going to take this second son away from you—a life for a life. After my son was born, until he was 18 years old, I literally spent every

day over controlling his life and obsessing about ways he would get hurt or die.

Erin shares:

> I was a major perfectionist with my kids. I would make sure my daughter was perfectly dressed and that her hair was styled just right. What I didn't realize until later was that I was trying to prove I really was a good mother—I didn't want anyone to think otherwise.

A woman was made to be a life-giver and a life-nurturer. She is a teacher and caregiver to her offspring. She can see herself in her children and get glimpses of their destiny. She is made to partner with the Creator of the universe in calling her child's identity and destiny forth. This is the spiritual DNA God has put into the creation He calls woman. When this core identity and essential role is ripped from her, it cannot be restored without divine intervention from the God who commissioned her as "mother" in the first place (Genesis 3:20).

You see, abortion is counterintuitive to the nature of what it means to be created as a woman, a mother, a wife, a friend, and one who influences. Abortion is now woven into her core identity. "It's not just something I had done to me—it's now become part of who I am." And with it comes all the attachments: guilt, shame, grief, fear, victimization, and so on.

Friendships

Her friendships with other women are also disappointing. "Why can't I be real with them, she chides herself?" "Why do I always have to wear my game face with everyone?" She feels especially conflicted when she's with her Christian friends. In her head, she knows she should be able to trust them with her secret, because, after all, if you can't trust your Christian sisters, who can you trust? But her spiritual pride and her fear of rejection keep her from taking off the mask and allowing the power of honesty and openness to define her friendships.

Sharon shares:

> For close to 30 years, it was one of the deepest longings of my heart, that desire to have real authentic friendships with other Christian women. I wondered what it was about me that caused my relationships to stall at a superficial level. Why did I never really connect with other women at a heart level? I watched as other young moms in my neighborhood and in my Sunday school class grew close, but I always felt as if I was on the outside looking in. Many times when I would get the courage to attend a Bible study or some other opportunity to connect, I would end up feeling invisible, hardly noticed, and certainly not pursued. If someone did show an interest in getting to know me, I immediately put on my mask of protection and carefully measured everything I shared so as not to be found out. There was a boundary I wouldn't cross when it came to

relationships. The result was years of carefully guarding my secrets and living void of authentic friendships and community.

Tina shares:

> Superficial relationships would definitely describe my life. I was managing all my relationships from the grid of my abortion-wounded heart. I lived in constant fear of judgment and abandonment. I always felt as if there was something missing in my relationships, and that was authenticity. But now I can be authentic and transparent in my relationships because I'm no longer living in fear of rejection.

Sheppard shares:

> That self-inflicted wound completely shut me down internally. I functioned and even excelled on the outside, pretending everything was okay and overachieving at life, but it was all to cover up who I knew I really was on the inside. I held relationships at a safe distance, fearing if people knew who I really was they wouldn't understand or accept me because of the choice I had made. It eventually became exhausting and miserable. I was desperate for relief and real relationships.

Can't Forgive Yourself

Many women who have had abortions believe God is out there somewhere. She may even believe He can forgive her. But she suspects that God is fickle with His forgiveness, so if she's not working hard to stay on His good side, she will forfeit all the good grace she has heard about. But even if God did forgive her, she's convinced she could never forgive herself.

Marie shares:

> I asked God over and over about a thousand times for forgiveness. I couldn't believe His redeeming grace would be given to me the first time I asked because my sin was too horrific. Satan had me crippled in the arena of forgiving myself. I stayed shackled in unforgiveness, bitterness, and anger because I thought I was my own judge and jury and could never be forgiven. At the Deeper Still retreat, I was able to totally accept Christ's forgiveness and lay down my idolatry of thinking my sin was greater than what Jesus did for me. Galatians 5:1 says that it was for freedom that Christ set us free. This finally resonates in my heart.

Debbie shares:

> I do finally believe that God has forgiven me, my baby has forgiven me, and now I can forgive myself. I can do that because what Jesus did for me was enough. Thank you for helping me see that.

Multiple Abortions

Different studies have indicated that about 50% of American women who have an abortion have had at least one previous abortion. I want to bring some understanding into what is happening in a woman's heart when she continues to believe that another abortion is her best option. There is no one-answer-fits-all way to look at this pattern of choosing death over life, but let me share the thoughts of a few women who have gone down that path. Both of these women have allowed Jesus to rescue them from this self-sabotaging cycle.

Maria shares:

> My biggest fear was fear of more abandonment, period. My dad disowned me when becoming pregnant with my first child at 15 years old. We didn't speak again until I was 17. I can remember that my first abortion was so scary. My second and third abortion took more time and thought, but I could perceive my conscience was changing with each abortion. I was a single mother of two children already, and I was fearful of what people would think because all my children would have had different fathers. My heart hurt each time, and pieces of my heart were breaking off a lot more each time. My mind was so foggy and dark at that time, and I can't remember anyone telling me this was a bad idea. I didn't have a relationship with Jesus of any sort, but I was aware each time that I was morally messing with God's plan.

My first step to healing was accepting Jesus Christ as my Lord and Savior. The second step was to pray and listen to Him about what I needed to do to please Him in my heart and life. The third step was opening up my heart and preparing myself to receive whatever He had in store for me. I had to be a willing participant and receive what He had for me at the Deeper Still retreat. I was wide open for Him, and He met me beyond what I could've hoped or imagined.

Karen shares:

When I found out I was pregnant for the first time at 19, I was afraid. The father of the child was out of the picture before I even knew I was pregnant. I was single and was abusing alcohol and drugs, and I didn't think I could raise a child by myself. And quite frankly, I didn't want to be responsible for taking care of a child and how that might affect my life. I was selfish. The decision to have an abortion wasn't that difficult for me, as I had believed the lies that it was just a clump of cells within me—that it wasn't a baby yet. Also, I did not believe in God—I was in darkness and didn't have a strong moral compass. I was put to sleep for the abortion, so I didn't experience the procedure. I woke up in pain from the cramping and then waited a bit until I was ready to go. I met my mom in the lobby, and we left. I was relieved when I walked out the door, as I thought my problem was solved. I didn't experience any obvious negative emotional effects from the abortion and went on with my life. It seemed pretty easy.

The second time I got pregnant, the decision to have an abortion was much easier, as I had done it before with no apparent complications (at least I didn't see them at that time). I once again was put to sleep and didn't experience the abortion procedure. Again, when I left the clinic that day, I was relieved because my so-called problem was once again solved. Afterward, however, my life would begin to fall apart and I began living more and more destructively, but because abortion was legal and it was my "right," I had no idea the abortions were, in large part, causing this depression and anxiety that was coming over me.

Because of the destructive and careless lifestyle that I was living, I became pregnant two more times, and for the same reasons I had the first two abortions, I chose abortion two more times. Sometime after the fourth and last abortion, I descended into such a state of depression, despair, and self-loathing that I just couldn't bear going on. I had become so numb inside. At times it felt as if I was an empty shell of a body walking around. I didn't want to live, but I was afraid to die. I still didn't believe in God and had always felt that when I died, I would be floating around in a dark outer space forever, with no one around. Total isolation from anything and anyone. That scared me. Because of the fear of dying and having just a smidgeon of hope to cling to, I reached out for help and eventually found God and learned about the forgiveness and mercy of Jesus Christ, which I so wanted.

Prior to becoming a Christian at about age 25, I developed obsessive-compulsive disorder (OCD) at the age of 21, which was not diagnosed as such until several years later. My subtype of OCD is in the form of intrusive harmful obsessive thoughts. And although I may have developed the OCD regardless of the abortions, I believe that the enemy used my past abortions to exacerbate the harmful obsessive thoughts that manifested in me from the OCD. I became fearful that I might harm a child; therefore, I wouldn't babysit my nephews and nieces, and I was terrified of having my own child for fear of harming them. Because I had taken the life of four of my children in the womb, the enemy ramped up his efforts to prevent me from having any children (made in the image of God) by enhancing the lie that I would harm my children. The lies in my head were strong and began before I became a Christian and before I began to learn the truths of God. Because the lies were so strongly embedded within me, I never ended up bearing a child. The biggest rip-off of my life was to first end the lives of my four children in the womb from abortion and then to never bear a child after that because of the lies caused by OCD and the devil.

But God!

At the age of 41, God called me to volunteer at a local pregnancy resource center to prevent others from making the same tragic choice I made. That's where my healing journey began. I went through a post-abortion Bible study at the center, and during the study, God moved the loss of my four children from my head to the depths of my heart. I now knew in my heart that they were real, and I gave them names (Stephen Michael, Joseph Ryan, Sarah Elizabeth, and David Uriah). Finally, after 20 years, I was able to grieve the loss of my children. I cried many tears, and one day, I cried such deep guttural groanings, the likes of which I'd never experienced or heard before. I was deeply mourning the loss of my children. It was difficult but necessary. The Lord did such a mighty work in me through the study, and now He was able to use me in ways I could never have imagined. I began facilitating Bible studies for other women hurt by abortion and began to speak out about its harmful effects and also the mercy and healing grace of Jesus Christ. At the age of 51, God in His loving mercy took me to a deeper level of healing at a Deeper Still retreat. I wasn't sure I needed more healing, but I decided to see if there was more healing to gain. Indeed, there was. God wanted more for me and more of me. The retreat was so beautiful and so powerful, and God gently took me to a deeper level of healing and into a deeper relationship with Him. After the retreat, I felt compelled to start a Deeper Still chapter in Southern California with my mom

> and others. What an honor and privilege to serve God and others this way. My relationship with God continues to grow deeper since that retreat, and God continues to use me in ways I could not have imaged. It's only by His grace—it has nothing to do with me. I just said yes to going deeper with Him, and He took it from there. What a good, good Father we have.

Moral Indifference

An abortion-wounded heart can manifest in myriad ways and at various levels of severity, but I want to take some time to highlight what could arguably be the most dangerous and deceiving of all manifestations.

I've heard and read many discussions and debates about abortion over the years. These points of view range from secular feminists to psychology experts to the sociological impact of abortion and then onto the medical risks or safety regarding abortion procedures. And if that weren't complicated, enough try digesting the vast and varying theological points of view concerning abortion and personhood. Not only are such discussions exhausting, they also can get so complicated and academic that you can lose sight of what we're really talking about.

This may sound simplistic, but I don't think that the essence of abortion and its effects are that complicated or esoteric.

How abortion and its aftereffects may or may not have impacted you, me, or anyone else doesn't prove or disprove anything. It doesn't matter if your abortion-wounded heart manifested in every possible symptom you've ever read or heard about or not—that's still not the basis upon which we judge the merits or horrors of abortion. Even if you legitimately never gave your abortion a second thought, never had a nightmare about it, or ever felt even a twinge of guilt, that still proves nothing about the rightness or wrongness of your abortion.

Abortion matters because God says it matters. And even if you don't believe there is one true God who has established certain moral laws that govern our spiritual and natural universe, it still doesn't take you off the moral hook. (Please hear me out before you throw this book across the room.) The Bible is so clear that the shedding of innocent human blood and particularly child sacrifice is an abomination to God because God created humans in His image and called them (us) sacred. He never gave humans authority to take the life of other innocent human beings.

It really doesn't matter how we feel about abortion, how we think about abortion, or how we analyze its aftereffects. Abortion is first and foremost a moral and spiritual sin against God and His creation. And even if we never manifest one negative effect from our abortion, the Bible teaches that we have innocent blood on our hands and we are therefore morally guilty for that innocent blood.

I want to emphasize this important truth because if it points to nothing else, it points to this: whether we feel it or not, we all share collective guilt in one way or another for the shedding of innocent human blood through abortion. Whether we personally obtained an abortion, coerced it, counseled for it, administered it, voted for it, legislated it, ignored it, or just culturally agreed with it, we are morally responsible before God for our choices, actions, inactions, and attitudes.

But here's the good news and the reason I wrote this book—we have a Savior! A savior is one who saves us from a situation where we cannot save ourselves. Jesus Christ is the one and only Savior whose blood was shed to pay the price for our bloodguiltiness. All we need to do to have that moral guilt atoned for is to repent and accept the payment that Jesus Christ made in our stead.

I believe that once we are assured that our moral guilt has been atoned for and we have accepted the only payment that will eternally count, then we are freed from the sin of moral guilt. Moral guilt is not an emotion—it is a spiritual moral condition. When you humble yourself before God and repent and take that step of accepting the payment that Jesus Christ bought for you, then that will become the most significant game changer of your whole life, and you will immediately be justified to start a fresh new beginning with a clean slate. Then your healing journey can begin.

Not only is this true from a spiritual legal position, but it's also true from a relational position. It was not a spiritual legal solution that motivated Jesus Christ to endure all the suffering, mockery, and dishonor that went into His crucifixion, but it was His great love for us that motivated Him to pay such a price. His love is that deep, wide, high, and eternal.

If you find yourself or someone you love in the pages of this chapter, please take courage! There is no shortage of grace or miraculous power available to you through the Lord Jesus Christ. Your wounds are not too big or overwhelming for Him. He paid a great price for your healing and for your freedom. But receiving His invitation to healing and lasting freedom is a choice only you can make for you.

My prayer is that you will choose life so that you may live free indeed. And not to just attain your own personal freedom, but that your heart can be expanded to receive Christ's passions in your heart. We need our hearts to break for what breaks His so that we can be about our Father's business and His Kingdom purposes for our lives and for the billions of lives He longs to reach.

Healing Exercise

This exercise is for anyone with an abortion-wounded heart—male or female.

The first step in gaining relief from the weight of moral guilt is to acknowledge your sin before God. God's invitation is not only to forgive you of your abortion(s) but to also give you eternal life. Listed below are scriptures from the Bible that reveal our need for salvation from our sins and of His free gift of eternal life. The first prayer is a prayer of salvation; if you have never fully surrendered your life to Jesus Christ, you need to start there. Following the salvation prayer is another prayer of forgiveness for your abortion(s) and the people in your story.

God's Love and His Plan for Us

> Jesus said, "I came that they may have life, and have it abundantly." (John 10:10)

And He will wipe away every tear from their eyes; and there will no longer be any death; there will no longer be any mourning, or crying, or pain; the first things have passed away. (Revelation 21:4)

Our Problem: Separation from God

For all have sinned and fall short of the glory of God. (Romans 3:23)

But your iniquities have made a separation between you and your God, and your sins have hidden His face from you so that He does not hear. (Isaiah 59:2)

There is a way which seems right to a man, but its end is the way of death. (Proverbs 14:12)

God's Remedy or Solution: The Cross

But God demonstrates His own love toward us, in that while we were yet sinners, Christ died for us. (Romans 5:8)

For there is one God, and one mediator also between God and men, the man Christ Jesus. (1 Timothy 2:5)

For Christ also died for sins once for all, the just for the unjust, so that He might bring us to God. (1 Peter 3:18)

Our Response

> For God so loved the world, that He gave His only begotten Son, that whoever believes in Him should not perish but have eternal life. (John 3:16)

> But as many as received Him, to them He gave the right to become children of God, even to those who believe in His name. (John 1:12)

> For by grace you have been saved through faith; and that not of yourselves, it is the gift of God; not as a result of works, so that no one may boast. (Ephesians 2:8–9)

Prayer of Salvation

Dear Lord Jesus,

Through your word and through revelation from your Holy Spirit, I can now see that I need a Savior. I cannot atone for my sins through my own efforts or by going through any religious motions that look like Christianity. I recognize that I need to stand before you alone as an audience of one.

Lord Jesus Christ, I come before you now and ask you to forgive me from all my sin and cleanse me by your blood. I now surrender my entire life to you and ask you to come into my life and be my Savior and the Lord of my life. Your Word says that by your grace and through faith in your finished work on the cross I have become a new creature in Christ. Your Word says that you are now my Abba Father and I am your beloved daughter/son. I now receive this truth and I thank you for this new identity.

As I leave my old life behind, I ask you to fill me to overflowing with your Holy Spirit. Make me a disciple of your Word, empower me with your Spirit so that I can walk in obedience to your word and ways. And I ask you to renew my mind, heal my heart, and help me to hear your voice—the voice of my Father. In the name of Jesus, Amen!

The next step to healing and lasting freedom is to extend the same forgiveness you have received from God to yourself and to others. As you chose to accept responsibility for your sins against others, your sins against yourself, and for the sins others have committed against you, then you no longer owe a debt and you no longer hold a debt. You are debt free!

The following is a prayer of repentance and release. You will insert the names of people and their sins as you pray through the prayer. You start by making a list of the people and their sins (their debt). We call this the *Certificate of Debt.* This comes from Colossians 2:14, which describes what Jesus did with our sins—*"having canceled out the certificate of debt consisting of decrees against us, which was hostile to us; and He has taken it out of the way, having nailed it to the cross."*

Next, make a list for these three categories for your *Certificate of Debt* (regarding your abortions):

1. Names of people and the sins you have committed against them.

2. The judgments you hold against yourself and the self-destructive ways you punish yourself.

3. Names of the people who sinned against you and what they did to you.

In the prayer below, you first pray to cancel your *certificate of debt,* and then the rest of the prayer is a declaration and a renunciation of your agreement with abortion and the evil spirits associated with it. This is an important step in gaining your freedom from spiritual oppression.

Prayer of Repentance and Release from Abortion and Judgments Against Myself and Others

God Releasing Me from the Debt of My Abortion(s) and the Debt I Owe My Baby(ies)

Dear Lord Jesus,

How can I thank you for so great a salvation? Thank you for this love that I can't even comprehend. Lord, I fully repent for the sin of my abortion(s). And I fully accept and receive your complete gift of atonement and forgiveness for my abortion(s).

I also acknowledge the great debt I owe my baby(ies) for taking his/her life and that I will never be able to pay this debt. Therefore, today I renounce all forms of self-atonement, and, in its place, I fully accept and receive that You, Jesus, have forgiven me and that You have paid this debt for me and that You declare over my debt, "Paid in Full!"

God Releasing Me from My Sin against Others

I now repent for my sins against (names) of (name your sins). And, today, I accept and receive that I am forgiven and that You, Jesus, have paid for my sins against these and that You declare over my debt, "Paid in Full!"

God Releasing Me from My Sins against Myself

I now repent for my self-punishing sins against myself of (name the sins), and I acknowledge that these are not pleasing to You, Lord. So today I renounce all forms of self-hatred and self-punishment. Instead, I now fully accept and receive that You, Jesus, have forgiven me and have paid this debt against myself and You declare over my debt, "Paid in Full!"

Releasing Those Who Sinned against Me

I bring before you (names) and their sins against me of (name the sins). I now accept and receive the payment that You, Jesus, made for their sins against me. Today, I fully forgive and release them from the debt they owe me, and I renounce a spirit of unforgiveness or bitterness toward these and I ask You, Jesus, to bless them according to your grace and mercy. I declare the debt they owe me is "Paid in Full!"

God Releasing Me from Satan's Grip

In the name of Jesus Christ, I repent of and renounce any alignments or agreements that I consented to or participated in with Satan, or with any evil spirits of murder, violence, death, false religion, witchcraft, or any other evil spirits as a result of my abortion(s), the shedding of innocent blood. Jesus, I now ask for your forgiveness and mercy for any access I gave the evil one, through abortion, in my life, my body, my soul, or my spirit.

And now, in the powerful name of Jesus Christ, and by His shed blood on the cross, I command any evil spirit who gained access to me—my body, my soul, or my spirit—to leave me now and never return, but go to the place where Jesus Christ commands you to go. I choose life, and truth, and place myself in complete agreement with the finished work of the cross of Jesus Christ. I take back all ground that I ever gave to the enemy through my abortion(s). I declare that my debts are "Paid in Full!"

Accepting Full Payment for My Bloodguiltiness and Breaking the Power of Shame

Dear Jesus, I now accept that your shed blood has removed my bloodguiltiness and has, therefore, broken the power of shame and the power of the accuser over my life and over my identity. I now renounce all spirits of shame, guilt, and accusation. And, in the name of Jesus Christ, I command these evil spirits to leave me and never return and go where Jesus Christ sends you. I declare that I am now free from guilt, shame, and accusation. I take back all ground I ever gave the enemy by believing these lies. I now ask you Lord Jesus to heal my memories and restore my identity so that I will walk in the knowledge of who you created me to be and who I am in You.

Thank you, Lord Jesus! Nothing I can do will ever be worthy of what you did for me. It is finished—and I receive it all!

Amen!

4

Abortion-Wounded Fathers

AFTER A FUNDRAISING BANQUET, one of our guests came up to me and said that in her entire life, she never once considered that a man would have any thoughts, feelings, or aftereffects from an abortion. This night was truly a revelation for her as she listened to a few of our male participants give their testimonies.

Unfortunately, this mindset is far too common, but it's not surprising. As I think back over the years of my life, the only men I've ever heard talk about abortion at all were either politicians or an occasional pastor. The only time I ever heard a man give a testimony about his aborted child was at a crisis pregnancy center banquet and then once or twice on a radio program.

When we don't hear from them, we just assume they've never given it another thought. I mean, how many post-abortive men are ever asked to be interviewed on a morning talk show? Or maybe just as shocking would be finding men who would be willing to tell their stories.

How grievous it is that the fathers of the millions upon millions of aborted children in this country have never been heard from. Equally so, how grievous it is that we have never given these fathers another thought regarding their heart in the matter? We've discovered through our Deeper Still retreats that abortion-wounded men aren't that much different from abortion-wounded women. We all have one thing in common: no one wants to talk about it.

However, there is one man who does want to talk about it, and His name is Jesus. Jesus sees the pain, the denial, the self-loathing, and the numbed-out hearts of abortion-wounded men. He wants to awaken them, heal them, and commission them into their God-ordained destiny. But the voice of Jesus needs to come through us, the redeemed.

In this chapter, I want to share stories from some of the brothers we've walked alongside as their fathers' hearts were restored. If you are a post-abortive man, my prayer is that as you get a glimpse into these men's journeys, you will find the courage to start your own journey to healing and lasting freedom.

Samuel shares:

> The abortion was a knife to my heart, cutting not only flesh but muscle, bone, and the heart itself. The lies I told were just clothing I kept over the wound. It was left unattended for years, and it festered and was slowly killing me. My new wife and I were pregnant when we got married. On our wedding night in a cabin in the mountains, we decided to have an abortion. Our plan was that she would call me at work and tell me she was spotting, just in case someone was listening. I would leave work, pick her up, and drive to the clinic. And that's what we did. Arriving back home afterward, I told my parents we had a

miscarriage. I've done some pretty horrible deeds in my life, but this one topped them all. Sometime later, our marriage ended.

The years went on, I remarried, and we were blessed with two daughters. But in 2012, things started to surface and come to a head. I developed an ulcer and started having panic attacks. On more than one occasion, my wife had to come to my work to drive me home. Eventually, the only place I felt safe was curled up in a ball in my bed. For days, I would lie in bed gasping for air as my wife slept peacefully beside me.

My first breakthrough came when a brother from my church came to visit me. I ended up confessing to him and sharing all I had done. He graciously listened, loved me, and prayed with me. I felt a huge burden lift off my back. But as time went on, I sank back down into my routine of just getting by day-by-day.

I had attended a Deeper Still fundraising banquet, and that night I knew I needed to attend a retreat. The panic attacks got worse, and, leading up to the week before the retreat, I had the worst panic attack yet. But as I made my way up the mountain to the retreat lodge, the fear was held at bay. The grace of God ushered me in to that retreat.

It's impossible to adequately relate in words what happened on that mountain or how the Lord revealed Himself to me, but the most precious and powerful thing He did for me was that He allowed me to see a vision of my son in heaven. All of the retreat participants were sitting on rocking chairs on the porch, holding the teddy bears that represented our aborted children. All of a sudden, the Lord opened my spiritual eyes and standing before me was a man, probably six feet three. His hair was short on the sides but thick and curly on top. It was the color of a brand-new copper penny. I kept remarking at how broad and strong his shoulders and chest were. He stood there, hands at his sides, head cocked to the side, and a smile on his face. He didn't say anything, but I knew instantly who it was. I said, "You're William—you're my son." He nodded.

Next, I could see a hand on William's shoulder. It was my father. He grinned his silly grin, the kind that didn't judge but instead put you at peace and almost offered a sense of humor. Then I saw another shadow on the other side of William, and it was my mother. I saw her face and her curly black hair. Here I stood, standing before the people I had let down the most in my life. I immediately wanted to apologize, but I knew there was no need to apologize. They held nothing against me. I started again to apologize for not giving William a chance. He let me know that he grew up with Christ as his father.

I cannot capture into words the joy that was felt on the mountaintop later that night as we all worshiped our God who had healed us. No amount of storytelling or prose will ever do justice when trying to explain what it's like for people who have lived in bondage for so long to finally find freedom

For a man, intrinsic in his spiritual DNA is the fathering instinct to procreate, protect, and provide for his children. God created fathers to lead their families to victory and destiny—not to have them sacrificed on the altar of an abortion table. A man's children may have been aborted by means of at least three scenarios:

- Without his consent or knowledge. This yields the highest level of feelings of powerlessness and helplessness (even if he wouldn't have wanted the child, it still goes against his leadership grid to not have a choice).

- He took the passive position of "It's your choice, and I'll support you in whatever you want to do." On the surface, this sounds supportive, but clearly, the message is "I'm not going to fight for you or for our baby."

- Through coercion, dominance, and force he pressured her into getting rid of his child. He could be a controlling, abusive person, or he could be under tremendous pressure from his family to make this crisis go away.

These scenarios all have varying degrees of consequence, but from the perspective of what brings life or death to a man's soul, all these scenarios emasculate men. Their God-given strength and courage to be leaders, protectors, and providers are exchanged for a passive capitulation to the demands of living in this world as a fear-driven survivor instead of a brave warrior.

William shares:

> I believed I had no influence or voice in the decision. I believed the lie that this decision was her choice alone, and so it happened that more than 30 years ago I stood by silently and waited while an abortionist took my child's life. It profoundly wounded his mother, destroyed a family, and stole my belief in who I was as a man.

His child was definitely denied his or her life, but what was this father denied? This father was denied making the kind of contribution that, in part, defines a man as a man. What is a father's contribution to his children or his family? It's things like his leadership, his heart, his problem- solving, his money, his reputation, his name, his fight, his love, his humor, his resolve, his wisdom, and his legacy.

Somehow, those kinds of losses are recorded in the soul of a man (no matter what his age) as a deep and significant failure. And it only reinforces the most feared answer to the question that every man asks of himself: "Do I have what it takes?" (*Wild at Heart* by John Eldridge). When he hears a resounding no to that question, he then accepts another layer of guilt, shame, and emasculation.

Scott shares:

> Then it was time. They led her away, and I could see in her face that she was so incredibly scared … I was so scared. I still clearly remember sitting

in a colorless waiting room, watching a mindless game show on a mounted wall TV. This was to be the entertainment for the men while their children were being murdered in the room next door. Every part of me was silently screaming out for help. I was sick to my stomach . . . I wanted to vomit. Just 20 feet away, my girlfriend was going through the most traumatic 30 minutes of her life. I wanted to run in and take her place and have them do it to me instead.

For the past 27 years, I have silently carried this decision, this wound, and this relentless memory. For 27 years, I have stuffed it, packed it, and locked it away—far, far, far away—simply hoping that over enough time and years it would finally be gone. There are times I can almost convince myself it didn't happen. But if I press in just a bit further, I can still see that stupid game show, and then I know it was all far too real and has become part of who I am.

As a man who fathered a baby who was aborted, I can simply share from my own experience that the abortion my girlfriend had deeply affected me and the trajectory of my heart in more ways than I wanted to admit. But God saw in me what I didn't want to look at until I trusted Him to take me to those places. At the Deeper Still retreat, He met me in the most profound ways when I let him in.

Bill shares:

When I chose to end the life of my child—not to protect his life, not to provide for his life—I made a choice to deny who God created me to be! I bought the lie that it was not my decision. I was deceived and denied my responsibility and my God-ordained purpose as a man. My heart and soul were damaged in a way that only God could heal and restore through the work of Jesus Christ on the cross!

My heart was broken when I first realized I was supposed to give my life for my child—not the other way around. At the Deeper Still retreat, God in His grace took me further than I knew I could go. He gave me wholeness where I didn't know that I was only half! He has strengthened my resolve, given me my voice back, and confirmed my calling to be a protector of life. I want to call men to attention and healing and to begin to walk in their God-given authority as fathers and leaders. It is my deepest conviction that God will not act to end abortion on the earth until men stand alongside women and acknowledge their sin before Him!

Jason shares:

It was more than 20 years ago that my girlfriend aborted our two children. I wanted to keep each one of them, but she felt differently. I left town the night before she had the first abortion. I went out into the woods and camped. The morning she had the first abortion—at the exact time of her appointment—I stood by the river, looking out over the water, and I heard a voice say to me, "You're damned. God had damned you." I felt a part of me die that day. The second one was just a few months later, and it felt much the same.

Over the years since that time, I struggled with addiction, anxiety, shame, anger, and health issues. I had trouble looking people in the eyes. Eventually, I prayed prayers of forgiveness, but deep down the disgust, the anger, the embarrassment, the rejection, and the shame remained. I didn't acknowledge the lives of those two precious children. I tried to pretend many times over that they never existed. I denied them over and over. I lived with this weight and secret for over 20 years.

Jason shares:

The retreat was one of the most incredible experiences of my life. I was finally able to share my secret in a safe place. I experienced the true love of Jesus and His peace deeper than I ever had before. I knew I was not damned. Instead, I was loved, accepted, and forgiven. I was finally able to embrace and acknowledge my two children, Ethan and Savannah. They became real to me. I know they're okay and they're waiting for me in heaven. One day I will hold them in my arms and kiss their beautiful faces.

When I went up that mountain to the retreat, I went up a grasshopper. I came down the mountain a giant slayer, a new creation in Christ. The anxiety, shame, and anger are no longer there. The parts of me that died more than 20 years ago were brought back to life. I got back my freedom to look people in the eye, and the voice I lost was restored.

Jerry shares:

As time went on, I began to think more about my past, including the child I had fathered that had been aborted. I still never talked with Kathy (my wife) about it. I didn't think she could ever understand, as she had never been exposed to the kind of lifestyle I lived. I began to experience lots of anger and anxiety, and I didn't want any close relationships, even with her. Without my even realizing it, the guilt of what I had been involved in was catching up with me. My inner anger manifested itself more and more often, and Kathy was often the recipient. I just couldn't understand what was going on. I was often on edge, and small things really set me off. I never once thought that any of this was related to the abortion.

There came a point when Kathy told me she couldn't live like this any longer and insisted I get help. So I started to see a counselor about my anger. He recognized that there was more behind my anger than had yet come to the surface. As he began to pray about it with me, suddenly, right there in front of my wife, my abortion story came out. I finally realized how deeply the abortion had gripped my life. It had deeply affected my thought life and had adversely affected my relationships with my family and others. It also had kept me distant from God.

It was this revelation that started my journey to healing. When I was finally able by God's grace to forgive them and myself for what happened to my little girl, there was a huge weight lifted off of me. The power of forgiveness was like nothing I have ever experienced in my life. The freedom I experienced was miraculous. I was free of the anger and the anxiety that had been with me for so many years. So the Lord had done a huge work in my heart even before I went to my Deeper Still retreat. But during that three-day retreat, the Lord took me to a depth of healing I never thought possible. He gave me the opportunity to finally allow my heart to receive that I have been spiritually reconciled with my daughter in heaven. I had a new ability to grieve for my loss, but I also have joy in the knowledge that we'll spend eternity together. On a mountaintop in Tennessee, I found a profound peace with my past, a new freedom for my future, and forgiveness and healing beyond anything I could have imagined. In just three days, my life was forever changed.

John shares:

> I knew before I went to the retreat that losing my child 20 years ago had made an impact on me, but I didn't realize how much of an impact it had on every aspect of my life. I have always dreaded the thought of meeting my child in heaven. I could only imagine myself falling down on my knees and begging him for forgiveness for allowing the abortion to happen. But as I brought all my fears, dreads, and regrets to the Lord that weekend, He began to cleanse, heal, and give me new eyes to see. Now I look forward to holding my son in my arms for the first time. I don't think my spiritual legs will allow me to run fast enough to get to him, nor will my spiritual arms be strong enough to hug him with the longing I have to see him.

William shares what the Lord revealed to him during his retreat about the spiritual battle that was being waged around him the day of his girlfriend's abortion:

> God took me back to that moment in the waiting room at the abortion clinic. He let me see what was taking place in the unseen spiritual realm. I saw an army of angels behind me with swords drawn ready to battle on my behalf. Their eyes were looking up to the Father—waiting on His command. The Father's eyes were on me—waiting for me to speak on behalf of my child and his mom. Demons were present, leading my girlfriend away. There was one moment for me to say, "Stop! Don't do this. We can work through

> this." I know now that's what she wanted to hear from me, but I was silent, and as she walked away, God raised His hand toward the angels, shook His head no, and they faded and disappeared.
>
> I saw the Father's heart being broken—but He never left me! In all those years of my healing journey, for the first time, I was seeing how deeply my sin touched God's heart, and I was broken open in a deeper way than I had ever know before. I had dealt with the deception, anger, and forgiveness in the past, but I'd never looked at the impact of my abortion on the Father's heart.

Indifference

There is another characteristic of an abortion-wounded heart that is subtle but could become the most crippling and paralyzing. It's an emotional and spiritual numbness and indifference regarding their abortion(s). It can cause the man or the woman involved to conclude that the whole thing really was not a big deal after all.

Shann says it this way:

> The only thing that really bothered me was that it didn't bother me.

It wasn't until he was willing to allow the Holy Spirit to begin to peel the layers of denial away from his heart that he could begin to recognize that these abortions he participated in were, in fact, his two daughters. Had he not submitted to the spiritual heart surgery Jesus was inviting him to receive, he would never have come to the place of truth and the freedom that comes when your heart is willing to look the truth square in the eye. You discover it's not the truth that's been your tormenting enemy all these years, but instead, it was your heart that condemned you, and those accusing demons only reinforced the condemnation.

When you know you can't fix your own heart, your only recourse is to deny your heart of what it really needs. Perhaps spiritual heart disease can be defined as those parts of your heart that have stopped beating. Your heart no longer receives the spiritual life-giving blood or oxygen it needs to survive and thrive. And the parts of your heart that are still beating require a tremendous amount of labor just to breathe.

When a man's heart has grown numb, he can't hear the beating heart of his children.

Shann shares:

> At my retreat, the Deeper Still team gave us an opportunity to receive a teddy bear as a tangible symbol of each of our aborted children. I sat in my chair as the bears were being unveiled on a table in the front of the room. The ground between me and that table was like the Great Divide. I was glued to my seat. You see, I knew that if I crossed that divide and took those bears in my arms, I would come face to face with the truth that I had shielded my heart from all these years. With more courage than it took to be a Marine, I walked up to the table and picked up my two bears. As I sat in the rocking chair and held them

> in my arms, my heart was breaking, and I felt Jesus destroying the barrier I had erected. For the first time in 23 years, my two daughters became real to me. And now I can't wait to meet them in heaven one day.

The truth sets you free when you know that the debt you can never pay has been paid in full by someone else. The only thing you need to do to remove your debt from heaven's ledger is to receive the payment. When that transaction happens, your heart will be reconciled not only with God but with your aborted children. When Shann submitted to this surgery, he came out of it with freedom, peace, and joy he never thought possible. He now lives with the truth that he will have all of eternity to get to know and love his daughters.

You see, in God's Kingdom, He makes all things new. It's not that God takes a giant eraser and removes all our choices and their consequences, but if we repent and cry out for His mercy, He will forgive our debts and begin to weave a new story in our life with a beautiful redemptive red thread from His own blood. The author of this new story has the power to bring beauty from the ashes. Who is a God like ours?

Questions for Reflection

For Women – I believe these are the challenges for us women:

Are we willing to think in a new way about the men who have participated in abortion?

If they have directly hurt us, are we willing to allow the supernatural grace of God to give us the power to forgive them?

Are we willing to make space in our hearts to extend compassion to the men who need a savior as much as we do?

Are we willing to let our brothers have a voice in this issue? Are we willing to support them as they give leadership in this battle for life?

For Men – I believe these are the challenges for men:

Are you willing to acknowledge that you were the father of your aborted children?

Are you willing to repent and bring your guilt, shame, and failure to the cross of Jesus Christ and receive His forgiveness and reconciliation?

Are you willing to seek reconciliation with the mother of your children (if possible and if the Lord opens that opportunity)?

Are you willing to be transparent with your heart and share how God has healed and restored your heart so that others can find that same healing?

Are you willing to let your voice be heard and give your strength and leadership in this battle for life and for the unborn?

5

Why Go Deeper Still?

KIM SHARES:

> I thought I had already found healing, was restored, and was ready to help someone else. I'm a clinical social worker after all—always eager to help, but always failing to deal with my own hurt or needs. I even told someone that I didn't foresee myself even crying during this retreat because I had already found forgiveness. Little did I know how deep I would be taken during this sacred weekend. Little did I know how many tears would fall from my eyes—tears as I worshiped freely for the first time, ever.

It's a Gracious and Glorious Invitation

God is ever inviting all of us into deeper places of spiritual and emotional health and intimacy with Him. Going to deeper places of healing does not negate any healing you've already gained. But it does humbly acknowledge that there may still be places in your soul that have not been made whole and have been preventing you from walking in your full destiny in God.

If you're a Christian, you know that receiving forgiveness and atonement for your sin can happen instantly if you have received it in faith and with a sincere heart. When this happens, it means that the debt you owed for the sin you committed has been canceled and wiped off heaven's ledger, because Jesus Christ paid it for you when He shed His blood on the cross. But in terms of forgiveness, the next level of healing and freedom is when you realize and accept that those who hurt you will never be able to pay the debt they owe you. No matter how much you wait for it or try to punish them (even if you're not aware that's what you're doing) it will never satisfy your soul.

Sue shares:

> For the first time, I was truly able to forgive those who had deeply hurt me, knowing the price Jesus paid was enough to not only cover my sins, but for theirs as well, and nothing they could do could ever repay me for the hurt they caused. But Jesus could pay it in full and He did.

Often, a woman who has had an abortion or a man who has fathered an aborted child has asked God for forgiveness, and on good days they believe He has. They may have even taken the next step and extended forgiveness to the others involved who hurt them. But after that's done, it is easy to conclude that they've fully dealt with their abortion and are healed. So they wonder, *Why would anyone suggest that I might need more healing?* The implication is, *I've done the work, and I've moved on, so you needn't ask me anymore.* After all, doesn't the Bible say we should press on toward the goal and forget what lies behind? Besides, what's done is done, and there's no good reason to bring it up again, right?

If you ask that same woman if she believes God delights in her and has good things in store for her, she will most likely hesitate to answer or even tear up if she thinks about it long enough. She may feel confident about getting into heaven someday, although she doesn't want to think about meeting her baby in heaven. But as far as this life, she figures that she has forfeited the good plans God had for her life, so she'll just do her best to get by and mind her own business.

Debbie shares:

> Even though I was a born-again believer, I felt as if I were a second-class Christian. Even though I knew Jesus forgave me, I still felt like I had a scarlet A on my head.

Catrina shares:

> Although I had asked for forgiveness and somewhat believed God had forgiven me, it lingered in the back of my mind always. If someone said the word, my insides would cringe. But now since I went deeper still, I am a new person every day. I find so much joy that I never had before, I love the people in my life so much deeper than I ever knew I could. I have joy! I wanted to shout it from the mountaintops, and, actually, I did one fall day last October.

If you asked an abortion-wounded man if he knows the purpose or vision God has made him for, or if he has something he's impassioned to defend, fight for, or protect, you can almost see in his eyes the defeated warrior who either maintains a false bravado to hide his feelings of failure, or you see the one who has dropped his sword. If you keep probing, he will begin to recount for you a trail of plans he had for his life but that never came to fruition. He's been living out his own self-sabotaging vow that says, "Success for me in this life has been forfeited."

Todd shares:

> I never spoke about my abortion for 16 years. It was placed deep down in a dark room where no one could ever go, including myself. I had prayed for forgiveness a thousand times, but it never seemed to help. One day, in a rare spiritual moment of courage, I shared my most painful secret with a friend from my church. This moment would begin my journey to healing, forgiveness, and freedom by leading me to a Deeper Still retreat. I realized I had believed some debilitating lies for all those years.
>
> I believed that God forgave me, but that it was an impersonal legal agreement. I knew that Almighty God forgave me through some legal binding spiritual contract He made with human beings. I could be forgiven and punch a ticket to heaven, but something life-giving was missing. He had to forgive me, but He did not have to like me or be for me.
>
> I assumed I had forfeited or was disqualified for any true abundant life realities. I had developed a self-sabotaging cycle in my life. If I

> became too successful or started enjoying any facet of life (relationships, accomplishments, job performance, etc.), I would do something to ruin it. I was not only uncomfortable in the first chair, I also felt I didn't deserve it. I would unconsciously do something stupid, foolish, or rebellious that placed me back down to a lower position where pressure and expectations were gone.
>
> The lie that kept me bound up was this: although I was forgiven for my sin, I was not released from the consequences of that sin. I needed to pay for it the rest of my life. Some Christians I have been around appeared to reinforce my disqualification for any significance in God's kingdom. The Holy Spirit showed me at the Deeper Still retreat that I was not only set free from my sin, but I was set free from the penalty of that sin. Jesus took them both.

Forgiveness and atonement for our sin is certainly one of the first steps in the journey to healing and restoration. But there can be quite a journey between having our debts canceled and walking free from shame and grief and living in lasting freedom and with hope for the future. Think of it this way: forgiveness is where the healing begins.

As broken people living in a fallen world and having an aversion to pain, we tend to want quick fixes. If we're in trouble, we want a quick way out. The whole abortion industry is built upon the false promise that it will all be over quickly. In a similar way, when a woman is seeking healing from her depression and anxiety because of her abortion, she's also looking for a quick way out. She hopes that when she asks God for forgiveness, it will also mean she would be instantly delivered from all the aftereffects of her abortion and it would be as if she never had the abortion in the first place.

Before I delve further into the fruit of deeper healing, let me be clear about something: it's not that God can't do a quick work, because He certainly can and does. By His sovereign grace, He can choose to instantly heal and deliver you from that which holds you captive. But I think the question pertaining to the length of time it takes to receive healing and restoration from an abortion is not so much about how long it will take—it's more about how deep you're willing to go. I have seen the Lord do a quick work when He's been given permission to do a deep work.

Sometimes people ask me if I think you can ever be totally healed from an abortion. My answer is yes, but with some qualifiers. There is one sense in which we still live in a fallen world, and we will always strive against the ravages of sin and its effects. But that doesn't mean we're doomed to be crippled until Jesus comes back.

Healing is Quantifiable

Healing is quantifiable. If I have a broken leg, then I can't walk. If my broken leg is healed, then I can walk again. If I build the muscles back up, I can even run a marathon. Wounds of the soul and spirit have similar dynamics. If you have an abortion-wounded heart, there may be many ways that it has emotionally and spiritually crippled you. But as you receive healing, you begin to experience freedom from the guilt, shame, and condemnation you once lived under.

Sometimes you don't even realize you were in bondage until you begin to experience freedom. When you're walking in freedom, it's easier to identify the bondages that once held you captive. It's like the blinders come off and you can see things that you haven't noticed before.

I've heard countless testimonies from our retreat participants who make statements such as, "The sun is brighter, the grass is greener, and nature just looks more beautiful." If you're focused inward because of your preoccupation with your own guilt, shame, and grief, then even the natural provisions God gives us to demonstrate His nearness—such as the beauty of His creation and the blessings of this life—will elude you.

So what does freedom from an abortion-wounded heart look like? For starters, you can now say the word *abortion*? It's a free day when you no longer get nauseated when the subject of abortion comes up or when you don't go running out of church when the pastor starts talking about abortion. How about when you can share your testimony without fearing the judgment of others? It's not that some people won't judge you, because there will always be people who will judge you, but when you're free, you no longer obsess about what people think of you.

When you are confident that the blood of Jesus was enough to cancel your debt, then you are free to openly share your story without fear of condemnation or the gossip of man.

Andrea shares:

> Since I received deeper healing, I'm able to attend a sanctity of life service without wanting to escape. When I see pro-life materials, such as

crosses and bumper stickers, I no longer feel the condemnation. I can look pastors and leaders in their eyes without shame or guilt.

Freedom means you can now think about your aborted baby as a person that God created and as separate from you. Until that point, your abortion has been more about your big mistake and shameful secret (that you feel obligated to hold on to) than it has been about the little person who God entrusted to you.

Freedom is emerging when you can begin to grieve your loss, because now you can finally name your loss. Your loss was not just the loss of your innocence, your relationship, your clean conscience, your dignity, your health, your hope, or your identity and self-worth (although those are all legitimate losses), but the quintessential loss from your abortion was your child.

And that loss was and is profound indeed. But glorious freedom is released when you can receive the peace of God that surpasses all understanding because you know that you have been first reconciled with God but also spiritually reconciled with your baby (Colossians 1:20). And when you can embrace this truth, you no longer need to dread or even hesitate when you think about meeting your child or children in heaven someday because now there is no wall of offense between you.

These are all glorious markers of God's grace and mercy. It's the Father's heart to see you reconciled and set free from your sin and brokenness. And beyond that, He commissions you to go forth and become a minister of reconciliation while it is still your watch here on earth (2 Corinthians 5:18–19). He still has good works for you to do

(Ephesians 2:10). When the gag order that the enemy decreed against you has been canceled and his clutches around your throat have been released, then you can get your voice back. And when you get your voice back, you're free to speak. And when you're free to speak, you can expose the truth about abortion and the death it brings on every front. You can become an advocate for the unborn and for others who have been wounded by abortion.

Icing on the Cake

Beyond the gift of freedom to live and function with core emotional and spiritual health and to have a restored hope for the future, The Holy Spirit can reveal things that would bring you more, peace, joy, or resolve. These could be gifts of revelation about your baby, a new perspective on your past, or a new understanding about your life from God's perspective. An example from my own life came during the memorial service at one of our retreats. I was waiting for the next transition in our program, when, seemingly out of nowhere, the Holy Spirit dropped a revelation into my spirit about my aborted child (at this point I only had the conviction that I had been pregnant with one child). Suddenly I understood that she was and is a worshiper and a worship leader in heaven. I understood that she had been gifted and endowed with a special gift of worship and that she was talented (as we would think of it here on earth) and that although we on earth were denied her and her gift of worship to God, she is now living out her eternal destiny leading worship with the saints. Well, Hallelujah, right?

This all took me by surprise because I was not focused on me nor was I asking God for anything like this. I was just there to serve my sisters, and He took me deeper still. For me, this was an icing-on-the-cake kind of moment. I did not necessarily need that revelation to function in freedom, but it sure was a huge blessing that gave me much joy. And it came because I was in a place where God's presence was strong, and my heart was joining with all those other ladies that morning who were willing and desirous to go deeper still.

Many of our participants have already experienced some level of healing before coming to a retreat. But most aren't even aware of what else God might want to touch and heal in their lives. But without a doubt, if they are willing to go deeper they all come through the retreat walking in new levels of healing, freedom, and hope for their future.

For you, deeper still may mean taking the first step in your healing journey. Maybe your deepest need at this point is just to experience the love and forgiveness of God. For another, you may be ready for the Lord to reset your whole sense of identity. If abortion becomes interwoven in your core identity, then your whole life becomes about managing your image and being acceptable to others. But when your true identity gets reset, then there is a new foundation upon which to begin healing your broken marriage or to finally put to rest that striving and driven-ness you are enslaved to because you're trying to be the perfect mom or dad.

Linda shares:

> For all these years, the memory of those abortions were all about my sadness, my pain, and my shame. I had some post-abortion counseling a few years ago, and I knew God had forgiven me and that those babies were in heaven, but

> because I was the one that decided to end their lives, I thought surely they also rejected me, so it was impossible for me to look forward to meeting them in heaven. At the retreat, for the first time in 42 years, I began to focus on them and their lives, not just my guilt, pain, and shame. For the first time in all these years, I was allowed an opportunity to grieve in a healthy way for the loss of my babies. This brought such a relief and a release in my soul. Now I not only know God forgives me, but I have experienced His comfort and have truly received His love. I also know that my boys are joyful—that they enjoy living in the presence of God continually and that one day we will be united with great joy!

This is Patricia's poem after she received forgiveness and healing regarding her aborted daughter. She was able to receive these words from the perspective of her daughter in heaven.

> Dear Mommy and Daddy, don't cry for me. I'm here with Jesus, safe in His love. Just wait til you get here and see what's above: the sparkle of diamonds, the glitter of gold; the face of my Jesus, I daily behold; I'm never sad. I never cry. I never ask my Jesus why.

Layer by Layer

Often healing and deliverance is a layer-by-layer process. Some demonic strongholds that get erected in your life will not come down until certain preliminary battles have been won. Your faith in God's love for you and your growth in trusting in His goodness will be tried and tested before you are ready for the next round of healing. Sometimes you need to reach certain pinnacles of victory before you are ready to step into the next battle for freedom. But how amazing is it that God is so gracious and patient and long suffering? He will afford us time and the experience of His faithfulness so that we are confident of His love and power, which makes us ready for the next deeper still step He has for us.

I initially believed that my aborted child was a girl, and I named her Brittany Grace and she is a gifted worshiper. I have embraced that reality in my heart for many years. But still something deep in my spirit was never totally resolved for me concerning my daughter. It's not that I had any condemnation or fear about my lack of deep resolve, but it's more like I had a question that wasn't yet answered.

From time to time over the years, I would pray about it but was content to let it be a mystery if that was better from God's perspective. But more recently, the fog around this mystery began to lift. The best way I can describe it is that I noticed breadcrumbs of revelation along my path, or maybe I was just finally able to see the breadcrumbs. They ultimately led me to a new revelation that I could not receive until now. Only recently have I come to believe I had aborted twins and that the other baby was a boy.

I obviously can't prove that I was carrying twins, and I won't know for certain until Heaven, but when revelation comes from the Holy Spirit, it's a "deep calls to deep" kind of experience. My heart is expanding to embrace this new reality, and it changes things. It causes me to ponder another level of loss—not only my personal loss but also a profound loss for this world. My sense is that both the children conceived in my womb are gifted worshipers. And although their eternal destiny cannot be stolen, their intended contribution to this world was denied.

But even this loss is not outside the bounds of God's ability to redeem. The living generation of my children's age are the most worship-hearted generation I have ever witnessed in my lifetime. God's worshipers will be raised up, and they will usher in the presence of the Lord as they seek Him and worship Him night and day until His return. The spiritual DNA of Deeper Still has as its foundation the heart of worship. We are part of a movement that cries out for the presence of God to manifest in our midst so that we can offer Him not only the worship He deserves but the worship that our healed and restored hearts long to pour out to Him. The worship legacy of my family heritage lives on through a whole generation of God worshipers, and I am blessed to be able to mother some of those who are part of this movement of God. I am humbled and in awe.

God's Healing Is Also Systemic

In an earlier chapter, I referred to the wounds of abortion as being systemic because they affect many other areas of your life, such as relationships, mothering, fathering, and identity. That same principle is also true about the Lord's healing grace—it is also systemic. His healing work spills over into other related wounds. For example, the wounds that made you vulnerable to choosing abortion in the first place probably started with the wounds caused by sexual sin. And the door that opened you up to sexual sin may have been a stronghold of rebellion.

You can be bound up by a whole network of sins and strongholds that you have given place to in your life. The sinful strongholds in our lives never come about in a vacuum. One usually opens the door to another. That's why as part of the Deeper Still retreat, we take time to repent of and renounce the sinful strongholds that would make you vulnerable to abortion in the first place.

To walk in lasting freedom from your past, you also need to sever the unholy bonding, attachments, or alliances you have formed with other people through sexual sin or other forms of idolatry. We call these attachments unholy soul ties. It's important to recognize that when strongholds get erected in your life, they will feed each other and reinforce each other.

The good news is that when a foundational stronghold, like that caused by abortion, comes tumbling down, then the foundations of the other strongholds in your life start to shake and dislodge. Before you know it, the whole house of deceptive cards can come tumbling down. When this happens and a new and stable foundation is established, then God can start to rebuild your walls, just like Nehemiah did around Jerusalem. You will begin to see a restoration from all that the locust has eaten.

If you give God permission, He will continue to do a deep and thorough work. It won't be overnight, and He will never overwhelm you with the process, but you can be assured that no one can restore a battle-ridden life like God can. He formed you in the first place and He is well able to restore you beyond what you ever thought possible.

My encouragement for anyone who has experienced the ravages of abortion is always this: Don't be afraid of an invitation to deeper healing. You have nothing to prove, and you have nothing to lose—except maybe more shackles. If you're too threatened by the invitation to go deeper still, then you're probably still being triggered by a lie, a stronghold, or a blackmail threat from the enemy.

Consider this: another way to view a deeper still invitation is as an invitation from your Bridegroom, the Lord Jesus Christ. His desire is for His Bride to be able to look Him in the eyes without shame, to dance His dance, to hear His voice, and to not be afraid to feel the passions of His heart. True and honest intimacy with God is not even possible unless your heart is free to love, to yield, and to receive from His bountiful bosom of endless grace, mercy, and love.

On this side of heaven, we can only imagine what that side of heaven will reveal, but I feel confident that once we pass through the gate and see Him face to face, we will fully understand the value of the precious grace that He offered us while still on earth but that we did not partake of because we were either too fearful, too prideful, or too distracted. Let's not deny Him the joy of His bride eagerly receiving all He has for her so that when that day comes of our home going or of His appearing, we will have made ourselves ready, without spot or wrinkle, confidently wearing our robe of righteousness and taking our seat in the great banquet hall of the lamb (Revelation 19:7,9; Isaiah 61:10; Ephesians 5:27).

Healing Exercise

Here are two healing exercises that will bring deeper healing to an abortion-wounded heart. If you allow your heart to engage in these exercises, you will find deeper healing. It is my recommendation that you find a trusted friend or two that will engage with you in these healing exercises.

Grieving and Reconciliation with Your Aborted Children

Your aborted baby's identity likely got lost in the circumstances and relational fallout surrounding the time of your abortion. From there, it's easy to develop a mentality that your aborted baby doesn't really exist. You can go for years without acknowledging the personhood of your child. Your grief, therefore, is hidden, undefined, and unresolved. But once you embrace the truth that your abortion wasn't just a physical surgical procedure but was, in fact, your child, then you are ready to face your true loss.

When you make time and space for your heart to grieve the loss of your aborted child (or children), then you are also honoring their existence. Your ability to grieve the loss of your baby redemptively requires the assurance that you have been spiritually reconciled with your baby. Only then can you grieve without guilt and shame. You need to grieve your loss from the perspective of the cross of Christ. At the cross, Jesus paid your debt in full. He took your guilt and shame upon Himself. Jesus Christ paid the price for you to be spiritually reconciled with your child, and He has not taught your child unforgiveness. There is joy in heaven when you receive this reconciliation.

> And through Him (Jesus) He reconciled all things to Himself, having made peace through the blood of His cross; through Him I say, whether things on earth or things in heaven.
> (Colossians 1:20)

I believe the Scriptures support that aborted children do exist and are safe with Father God in heaven. Here are a few scriptures that reveal God's merciful character to provide for us when others forsake us. He created us not only with a physical body (that will only serve us in this life), but He gave us a soul and spirit that will exist eternally; plus, we'll all get a new body. He is both a righteous and merciful judge.

> Though my father and mother forsake me, the Lord will receive me. (Psalm 27:10 NIV)

> But now he is dead. Why should I fast? Can I bring him back again? I shall go to him, but he will not return to me. (2 Samuel 12:23; *This refers to when King David was grieving over the baby he conceived with Bathsheba after the baby died.*)

> And the dust returns to the ground it came from, and the spirit returns to God who gave it. (Ecclesiastes 12:7)

> It is sown a natural body; it is raised a spiritual body. If there is a natural body, there is also a spiritual body. (1 Corinthians 15:44)

> The Lord works righteousness and justice for all who are oppressed. (Psalm 103:6)

We have discovered that grieving your child comes easier when you have a tangible symbol to hold. At our Deeper Still retreats, we give our participants a teddy bear as a symbol of their aborted baby. We wrap them in a blanket and put a ribbon or a bow tie on them to signify a girl or boy. We invite the mothers and fathers to pick up their bears and sit on the rocking chairs on the porch. We give them time and space to hold, caress, cry, and receive comfort. They release grief and they receive comfort from the loving presence of Jesus and from the Holy Spirit that comforts us in all our brokenness.

I encourage you to engage in a similar exercise. It may feel awkward at first because you have not allowed your heart to be open to this level of truth, reconciliation, and healing, but there will be grace if you take the first step. You may also receive a name for your child or other impressions about them.

Restoring Your Mother Mantle or Father Mantle

Mothers and fathers of aborted children do not embrace their identity as mother or father with full honor. Part of your mother's heart or father's heart was aborted too. As a result, your living children are missing a part of *mother* and *father* that they desperately need.

Children cannot be nurtured or parented properly if mom and dad are running from their stewardship as parents because of guilt, grief, and feelings of unworthiness. Crippled parents tend to either push their children away or to smother them. Children need healthy bonding and healthy boundaries to feel secure their own identities.

Common Struggles

The following are common struggles for mothers and fathers who have abortion-wounded hearts.

Detachment

Detachment results in difficulty emotionally bonding with your living children. It might be particularly noticeable with the first born after the abortion. Your emotional detachment can also diminish physical touch with your children.

There are many cases of siblings of aborted children (especially those who were born next after the abortion) that find it difficult to bond and are more prone to fear and insecurity. Many have testified to "premonitions" of other siblings.

Katie's struggle:

> When I look into their eyes, I catch myself wondering if their sister would have looked like them. It feels unfair to lavish all my love and affection on my living children when their sister never had that chance. So maybe it's just better if I withhold from everyone.

Compensation

Compensation is a common reaction to personal guilt. It's trying to make up for that which you denied someone or for your failures. You give your children a lot of material things to make them happy but end up withholding relationship or discipline because it triggers guilt. It's easier to give material things than to step into painful emotions. You also feel the need to prove that you're a good mother or father by overachieving or overprotecting.

David's struggle:

> I work so hard, but I never feel like a good father. I try to meet all their needs and make sure they're safe, happy, healthy, well fed, well educated, and well entertained. It's like I'm trying to prove to my children that I really am a good father and that I won't hurt them.

Anger and Resentment

Siblings can sometimes become the unintended targets of anger and resentment stemming from the abortion and from a broken relationship with the father or mother of the child.

Shawna's struggle:

> I'm mostly angry and resentful of everything they do. It wouldn't be like this if their father didn't make me abort their brother.

Infertility

If abortion has contributed to the inability to have other children, a woman may shut down her mothering instincts and deny everyone the nurture and love that only she can bring.

Ruth's struggle:

> I never really wanted children anyway, besides, my dogs are a lot less trouble.

Expected Retribution

Your abortion may lead you to expect that something bad is going to happen to you or your family as retribution.

Tammy's struggle:

> I know God has given me a second chance, but if I mess up this time, I know He'll take one of my children.

If you are a post-abortive woman, the Lord wants to restore your mother's heart so you can embrace your calling and stewardship to mothering. I refer to this as your Mother Mantle. God has called you to wear your mother mantle with honor and courage. He wants you to be free to walk in healthy relationships with your living children and without fear of retribution.

Whether you ever bear natural children or not, God has designed you to mother. Your nurturing touch, wisdom, and kind words of instruction can help shape the identity of an emotionally neglected child. When your mother mantle is intact, you can bring comfort to the emotional orphans of this world who suffer from a profound mothering void. And remember it's not just children who are lacking the nurture and stability of a mothering influence in their life. It may be your co-worker or friend.

If you are a post-abortive man, the Lord likewise wants to restore your father's heart so you can embrace your calling and stewardship to fathering. Your Heavenly Father wants to awaken the defeated warrior in you. He wants to breathe His own Father DNA into your spirit. He wants to give you a new heart and restore your courage and confidence as a protector and provider. You are the one who gives your children your name and calls forth their destinies. Strength and authority are woven into the fabric of your Father Mantle. In a society and culture of the absent father, your wise instruction, playful attention, and courageous moral character can rescue the emotional orphans of this world from a fatherless abyss.

The deeper still invitation that Father God is extending to you women and men who have been hindered in your mothering or fathering is a new beginning to take up your Mother Mantle and your Father Mantle.

In a Deeper Still retreat, we use symbolic props to minister these truths. I encourage you to do the same. For the Mother Mantle, we place a regal robe on our women. It represents the beauty, creativity, and courage it takes to mother. You need to ask two or three women who are mature in their faith and mothering to place this robe upon you and pray for your mother's heart to be healed and restored. There are many people waiting for a mothering touch that is uniquely yours.

> Strength and dignity are her clothing and she smiles at the future. (Proverbs 31:25 NASB)

For the Father Mantle, we use a staff that represents a father's leadership and authority and a sword that represents his warrior spirit. You need to ask two or three men who are mature in their faith and fathering to lay hands on you while you hold the staff and sword. They will pray for your father's heart to be healed and will commission you into fathering. There are many people waiting for your fathering blessing.

Like arrows in the hand of a warrior are the children of one's youth. Blessed is the man who fills his quiver with them! He shall not be put to shame when he speaks with his enemies in the gate. (Psalm 127:4–5)

6

What's in a Name?

IN THIS CHAPTER, I want to help you see the power of a name to validate personhood. This is particularly important in the abortion debate because the denial of personhood is what makes people feel justified in aborting babies. We will see, however, that receiving a name is God's idea, and it's fundamental to affirming our personhood.

Have you ever given much thought to the idea that the whole concept of names or naming something or someone comes from God? It's so easy to take foundational truths for granted when they've always been there or have always been a part of our existence. It's kind of like oxygen. It's always been there, and we don't know our existence apart from oxygen, so we just breathe it in and go on about our business. We don't necessarily stop to ponder the origins of our oxygen or to thank our Creator for His magnificent design and provision for sustaining life.

God either directly gave names to His creation, or He delegated authority to His pinnacle creation, man, to give names. Consider the following Scriptures:

> He determines the number of the stars; he gives to all of them their names. (Psalm 147:4) Can you bind the chains of Pleiades or loose the cords of Orion? (Job 38:31)

> Now out of the ground, the Lord God had formed every beast of the field and every bird of the heavens and brought them to the man to see what he would call them. And whatever the man called every living creature, that was its name. The man gave names to all livestock and to the birds of the heavens and to every beast of the field. But for Adam there was not found a helper fit for him. (Genesis 2:19–20)

> The man called his wife's name Eve, because she was the mother of all the living. (Genesis 3:20)

> For this reason I bow my knees before the Father, from whom every family in heaven and on earth is named. (Ephesians 3:14–15)

Let's consider names for a minute. For one thing, God gave names to distinguish one thing from another. But names have meaning beyond identification or classification. Names are substantive. They can communicate character, personality, destiny, and personhood. Think about how strange life would be without names. Here's an example from the Bible when Joseph, Jacob's son, named his sons Manasseh and Ephraim:

> Joseph called the name of the firstborn Manasseh. For he said – "God has made me forget all my hardship and all my father's house." The name of the second he called Ephraim, "For God has made me fruitful in the land of my affliction. (Genesis 41:51–52)

Most old alien movies I've ever watched (or suffered through, to be more exact) had certain predictable traits. They had grotesque-looking creatures that somehow transcended mere humans. They always had a higher level of intelligence, they always had more power and more sophisticated technology, and they always had evil intentions toward humans. But, interestingly, these aliens never seemed to have names, and because they didn't have names, it was easy to keep viewing them as impersonal enemies without souls.

Interestingly though, the Bible records that even demons have names, and Satan himself is known by different names. These entities are clearly our enemy, but they too, have been given names by God.

> The name of the star is Wormwood.
> (Revelations 8:11)

> It is only by Beelzebul, the prince of demons, that this man casts out demons. (Matthew 12:24)

> Jesus then asked him, "What is your name?" And he said "Legion," for many demons had entered him. (Luke 8:30)

Just to keep our perspective on who's who, let me highlight one more name:

> Therefore, God has highly exalted him and bestowed on him the name that is above every name, so that at the name of Jesus every knee should bow, in heaven and on earth and under

> the earth, and every tongue confess that Jesus Christ is Lord, to the glory of God the Father. Amen! (Philippians 2:9–11).

God also created numbers, and the universe is filled with numerical intelligence and design. However, numbers do not have the same power or empowerment as names. Numbers lend themselves to efficiency. Numbers are not sentimental, nor do they evoke endearment or compassion as they are called out. If you go to the DMV or to the Social Security office, they are not as interested in your name as they are your number.

Ever since the massacre of 9-11-2001 in the United States, every year on that day the names of almost 3000 people who were killed are spoken out loud to honor them. They don't just speak out a number—they speak out a name. The power of the Vietnam memorial in Washington DC is not because there are 58,318 numbers engraved in granite for everyone to come and memorialize. The power is in the names. Personally, I don't know any of those people whose names are on that wall, but every time I visit it, I cry.

Whenever we want to create emotional distance from a person or an animal, we either don't give it a name or we don't call it by name. I recently read of a man who was a prison inmate. As long as he was a prison inmate, he was identified as inmate # ___. It's easier to treat someone inhumanly if they are a number without a name. If you visit a zoo, you will notice that these animals have names. If a child introduces you to his pet, the first question you're probably going to ask is, "What's its name?" But I'm guessing that the cows being raised in the stockyard that will eventually end up on your dinner plate are not given names at their birth.

Let's bring this discussion down to human babies who are aborted. The bottom line is that it's easy to abort a product of conception, and it's not easy to abort a person with a name. Everyone involved in an abortion has at least one thing in common. Whether you're the woman herself, the boyfriend, the parents, the doctor, the nurses, the receptionist, the lawmaker, or the supreme court judge, it's just easier for everyone involved if we can all agree to call the contents in her uterus just that—"uterine contents," "product of conception," or "blob of tissue." If we can stick to these terms, then we can keep it dehumanized and, therefore, emotionally irrelevant.

If this "product of conception" did not have a human soul and was not knit together in its mother's womb, and if it did not have physical and spiritual destiny already written on its DNA, and if it did not have heaven's stamp of approval that declares the *imago Dei*, then this whole abortion discussion would be moot and there would be no controversy. I contend that it's only controversial because we're dealing with more here than a biological mass. Let's examine a few more Scriptures from the Bible that opens our understanding of how God views and values His pinnacle creation.

> Can a woman forget her nursing child, that she should have no compassion on the son of her womb? Even these may forget, yet I will not forget you. Behold I have engraved you on the palms of my hands. (Isaiah 49:15–16)

> But now thus says the Lord, he who created you O Jacob, he who formed you, O Israel: Fear not,

> for I have redeemed you; I have called you by name, you are mine. (Isaiah 43:1)

> And behold, you will conceive in your womb and bear a son, and you shall call his name Jesus. (Luke 1:31)

> Do not be afraid, Zechariah, for your prayer has been heard, and your wife Elizabeth will bear you a son, and you shall call his name John. And you will have joy and gladness, and many will rejoice at his birth, for he will be great before the Lord. And he must not drink wine or strong drink and he will be filled with the Holy Spirit, even from his mother's womb. (Luke 1:13–14)

> And when Elizabeth heard the greeting of Mary, the baby leaped in her womb. And Elizabeth was filled with the Holy Spirit, and she exclaimed with a loud cry, "blessed are you among women, and blessed is the fruit of your womb! And why is this granted to me that the mother of my Lord should come to me? For behold, when the sound of your greeting came to my ears, the baby in my womb leaped for joy. (Luke 1: 41–44)

Did you notice that Jesus' mother was given His name before she had conceived Him? And Zechariah was given the name of his son, John, before he was conceived.

Names have a way of bestowing identity, honor, dignity, and destiny on us. Try to imagine a cemetery of gravestones without names. When you visit a cemetery, you don't see faces, you see names. Names carry the power of personhood even if you're just reading about them in a book.

When it comes to healing the abortion-wounded heart, a name for your child becomes an important part of the process. But there are some complex layers to this discussion, so let's try to peel off one layer at a time.

People with abortion-wounded hearts who are ready to acknowledge that something is not right in their soul will easily name at least three primary emotions that haunt them: guilt, shame, and grief. I certainly would have named those three, but, to me, they felt deeper than just emotions; they became more like conditions of my heart.

Guilt: A moral condition that produces guilty feelings. When we break one of God's moral laws, we feel guilt because we are guilty. The human soul was not created to carry the weight of moral guilt. We can't just brush it off. It requires a recompense, an atonement, or a punishment.

Shame: It's the companion of guilt and part of the consequence of moral guilt. Shame kind of feels like it sounds. It's heavy, it's slimy, it covers you, and it's full of accusation. Shame begins to redefine you and tries to tell you who you are and who you are not. Shame is demanding, and, eventually, it intertwines with your personality and tries to convince you it's just part of who you are, so just accept it and move on.

Grief: Unspecific grief is like a dreary day. There's a constant drizzle to it, but it never really ends; unlike a storm that comes in with thunder, lighting, and rain. It does what storms do and then it leaves. And once it moves on, the sky clears and the sun comes out. Grieving that is not redemptive or tied to a specific loss will not go away but will turn into a lingering depression and despair.

Guilt, shame, and grief can rotate like a vicious tornadic cycle. Until this vicious triad is broken apart, it will never dissipate. For an abortion-wounded heart to be freed from this vicious triad, there first needs to be a spiritual reconciliation with God to remove the moral guilt. When this happens our hearts are cleansed, softened, and submitted to God. This is how our heart gets circumcised. And just like the Lord promised the children of Israel in Joshua 5:7–9, He said after they crossed the Jordan and were circumcised, God would roll away the reproach (or shame) of Egypt from their hearts.

When you are carrying guilt and shame from an abortion, your grief can never be legitimized or validated because it is muddled in with all that guilt and shame. Therefore, you can never experience pure grief. But once your conscience has been cleared of the moral guilt and once your reproach and that stifling shame have been washed away, then you are free to acknowledge your loss. You can then recognize that your loss was not a just blob of tissue but a baby, and not just any baby, but your baby.

What an amazing gift that Jesus Christ has given us through His sacrifice and suffering. He made a way to pay for our debt, change our heart, reconcile our relationships, and validate our losses. But He doesn't just validate them—He heals them. His compassion is deep and wide and able to absorb our pain. He is the God of all comfort. He longs to comfort us in our losses. Through Him, we can experience redemptive grieving.

When our abortion-wounded grieving is redemptive, then we are empowered to give back to our children—not from a place of guilt but from a place of moral clarity and selfless honor. We can now see them from the new vantage point of a restored heart. We can give them our mother's or father's blessing, and we can give them their names. We can bless them with the honor and dignity of a name. Think for a minute about all the orphaned aborted children who have left this earth and have entered heaven's gates without a name or an identity from their parents.

When Scott came to our retreat, he had the assurance that God had forgiven him for aborting his daughter many years ago, but he had no idea how much deeper the Lord wanted to take him in freeing his heart so that he could actually look forward to meeting his daughter someday in heaven.

Scott shares:

> I imagined that I would get to heaven someday and it would be like a meet and greet session, and I would be going around introducing myself to everyone and saying "Hi! I'm Scott. What's your name? Nice to meet you." And then I would come to this girl about 27 years old and would say, "Hi! I'm Scott. What's your name?" And she would look at me and say, "I don't have a name, but you were my father."

This was the fear and pain that Scott had to bring to Jesus. On that day, Scott allowed his daughter to become real in his heart in a redemptive way. She no longer had to represent part of a "bad dream" to him. That day, he was able to embrace her as her father. That place of unresolved grief and loss was now being replaced with a new anticipation for a joyful reunion in heaven—not with a nameless, faceless, ghost that haunted him but with a beautiful, eternal daughter named Kayla Grace.

The price Jesus paid on the cross was big enough for that kind of redemption.

Most of the women I've walked with through this healing journey and who have taken these steps can easily embrace that their child deserves a name. And once their hearts are clear of guilt and shame, they can usually "hear" a name, and what beautiful names they are. Here are just a few to remind us that these people await us in heaven: Isaiah John, Jade and Michael, Isaiah, Zach and Bethany, Hannah, Amy Hope, Xavier Andres, Clinton Timothy, Molly Anne, Christina Rose, Laurel, Jamie Lynn, Amy, Daniel, William, Mary Grace, Harper Elyon, Piper Leesan, Joshua David, Brett Ashton, Jack Dylan, Brittany Grace, and James.

Once we started inviting the men—the fathers of aborted children—to our healing retreats, a whole new level of understanding and beauty began to unfold concerning how they viewed naming their children. Like in the examples above, when mothers name their children, they usually give them a first name and a middle name. But often when the fathers named their children, they included their last name.

When I first heard this, it shook me to my core. It never occurred to me how powerful it is for a man—for a father—to bestow his family name on his children. Part of his identity and his namesake is attached to his children in a way that completes their identity and is different from how women think about their children's identity. To hear these fathers give their family name to their children has brought profound healing to many women just by witnessing these men "legitimize" their children with their last name. For many post-abortive women, the father of their child never laid claim to their aborted child, so there was never a familial legitimacy given to their child. This, too, is a reality worthy of our grief.

When Mike came to our retreat, he was carrying years of stuffed away guilt, shame, and grief over his aborted daughter. He knew God had forgiven him, but he didn't really know how to get beyond forgiveness. When we reached the point in the retreat where we invite our participants to choose a teddy bear as a tangible symbol of their aborted baby, Mike at first felt paralyzed.

He watched others pick up their bears, but he kept hesitating. He had identified which bear was his, but it was as if he were glued to his chair. He then started contemplating what he would do if someone else took his bear. The Lord had to do something to get him up and out of his chair.

Mike shares:

> The Lord enabled me to hear in my spirit the heart cry of my daughter in heaven, "Daddy, come get me." That was all it took. I immediately jumped out of my seat and got to that table and picked up my bear. Her name came to me the night before when I asked the Lord to give me her name: Susie Snow Sneed. But when I picked up the bear, another level of her reality hit me. I then took her on a walk. I asked for forgiveness, and I talked through all the stages of this life that we missed together: her birth, first day of school, prom, graduation, wedding, grandchildren. It felt as if Jesus was being her advocate and that as I was confessing and asking for forgiveness, Jesus

> was reconciling us, and I was then able to legitimately lay claim to her as her father and give her my last name. My father's heart was finally at peace knowing that we had been spiritually reconciled here on earth, but we will begin our eternal relationship in heaven.

Jerrod Roberts also had a daughter who was aborted. It had been some years earlier, and Jerrod had already received some depth of healing regarding his daughter.

Jerrod shares:

> I had given her a first name and a middle name, but it wasn't until my Deeper Still retreat that I realized I never felt worthy enough to give her my last name. But once my heart was set free from that shame that had been between me and my daughter, I was able to give her my last name, which was now her last name. I can now honor Destiny Marie Roberts with her full name.

How beautiful that God is restoring the hearts of the fathers to their children (Malachi 4:6)!

The National Memorial for the Unborn is located in Chattanooga, Tennessee. One of the reasons this memorial is so powerful is because the ground it's built on used to be an abortion clinic where thousands of preborn babies lost their lives. In 1993, it was made into a memorial to honor aborted children from all over the world. Part of what makes this memorial so powerful is that it displays brass plaques on its big granite wall of names. On these plaques are written the names of aborted children. In addition to the names, there are also dates and phrases or epitaphs to honor these children.

Here are a few:

> Ava Marie: "In my dreams, I pick you every time."
>
> Ora Ben Haley IV: "My only child, I think of you every day!"
>
> Grandbaby King: "I miss you, I will hold you in Heaven"
>
> Shancey Irwin: "With all our love—Mom and Dad"
>
> Ashley Nicole Carr: "We love and honor you"
>
> Elijah James: Espeland Papa "Luv WJE & SLP"
>
> Kylie Olivia: "Born into heaven, held by Jesus"
>
> Juanita: "God's Gracious Gift" "Grace Saved A Wretch Like Me"
>
> Ebenezer: "The Stone of Help, Once Was Lost, Now I'm Found"
>
> Sable: "Third Born Child—God's Heir, Love & Mercy Found in Jesus"
>
> Uriah: "My Light Is Jehovah, My Many Sins Brought to Light"
>
> Sondra: "Helper of Mankind, No Longer Blind ... Forgive Me!"

Some of these plaques are signed by the mothers, but many are not. As you read through them, you can sense that, for many of these children, their mothers or fathers have not been able to acknowledge their existence. So many have had family members or friends who have stood in the gap for these little ones and have bestowed names on them.

The first time I visited the National Memorial for the Unborn, I was taken aback by how deeply it affected me. I knew it was going to be profound, but I think I was surprised by how strongly I felt the presence of Jesus. Even as I first stepped over the threshold before I even got to the wall of names, tears began to well up in my eyes. I knew I was on holy ground. As my husband and I walked into the room of the wall of names, it took my breath away. We spent the next hour just silently reading the names and the epitaphs and looking at the letters and gifts people had left on the granite shelf.

I think the reason I sensed Jesus' presence so strongly that day was because He was and is so pleased that a group of people took the time, money, and effort to create a space and a place to honor those children that the world discards without a second thought. In Jesus' eyes, these children have names and identities and are now full of eternal destiny.

These children were not war heroes. They didn't accomplish some major feat the world would acclaim. They did not even die from a disease where family and friends spent many long hours in the hospital praying for them and loving them before they had to finally let them go. The only thing these children brought to their existence is that Father God created them and began to knit them together in the womb of their mothers here on earth. From our perspective, they were a liability, but from heaven's perspective, they were full of destiny. I think that's why the affirmation of Jesus' presence is so strong in that little plot of land in

Chattanooga. It's because some of God's people valued these children that were heaven sent but earth rejected and saw to it that they could be honored by displaying their names.

The Bible says in 1 Corinthians 2:14,

> "The natural person does not accept the things of the Spirit of God, for they are foolish to him and he is not able to understand them because they are spiritually discerned."

1 Corinthians 1:27-29 states,

> "But God chose what is foolish in the world to shame the wise; God chose what is weak in the world to shame the strong."

Aren't you glad you were honored enough to have been given something as simple as a name? If you have a name, you matter. Isaiah 43:1 says God calls us by name. Have you ever read the pages and pages of genealogies in the Bible? I know they have historical significance, but I wonder if the Lord had all those names recorded so that we, millennia later, would understand that these were real people that made Biblical history and the Lord knows them all by name.

We are not some random existential biological composite that emerged out of nothingness. By no means! We were created by a faithful and intentional Heavenly Father who knit us together in our mother's womb, who breathed into us the breath of life, and who dignified us with a name.

Healing Exercise

Naming your children – If you are a mother or father of an aborted child or children, take time to ask Father God for their name. It may take some time, but as you open your heart, your ears will also open to hear their name. You may also want to honor them by getting a plaque with their name on it at the National Memorial for the Unborn: www.memorialfortheunborn.org

7

The Abortion-Wounded Church

"MAYBE YOU SHOULDN'T BE SO HARD ON YOURSELF." These were the words I heard coming from the pastor I had just confessed my abortion to and to whom I had just poured out my heart. His response initially left me feeling stunned. I'm sure I had a puzzled look on my face.

But within seconds, I could feel my soul shrinking back like a wave that recedes from the shore. I was expectant or hopeful that my desperate heart would receive some profound morsel that would have satisfied my hunger for relief. But what I got felt like a sip of sugar water.

It had been a couple of months since my abortion, and I was trying to process it all internally by myself. I would have liked to bring a friend or spiritual authority into my inner world, but I didn't know who or how. Plus, I was aware of this cloud of shame that was now overshadowing my mother. She was fighting her own battle and was feeling responsible for my every internal tear. She and I did not talk much about it during those days. I was trying to protect her, and she was trying to protect me, so we mostly kept our tormenting secrets to ourselves.

I knew my mother was seeking spiritual and emotional relief because she would call 1-800 prayer lines. She would pour out her heart to strangers over the phone, who would pray for her. I was thankful that she did that, but it also showed me how desperate her struggle was to get relief from the guilt, shame, and responsibility she was carrying. It was my mother who suggested that we go talk to a pastor together. I didn't object, but at that time I was doing it more for her than for myself. She made an appointment with a pastor several towns away.

It takes a lot of emotional willpower to pour out your story to a stranger. But when it's a pastor, you have certain expectations that he will give you the words of life that your desperate soul needs to hear. Now, in this man's defense, my mother and I had no relationship with this clergyman. Our shame-filled, abortion-wounded hearts would not dare seek out a spiritual shepherd that knew us or was invested in our spiritual health. We took the cowardly path of anonymity, hoping we would find the words of life we needed from a random man with a collar.

After he told me I shouldn't be so hard on myself, he then said that the church (referring to his denomination) had not yet taken a position on abortion. The implication was that abortion is a gray area, so don't jump to any self-condemning conclusions until we get this thing figured out. I was a 22-year-old heartbroken young lady, grieving and feeling as if I'd forfeited all the good things God had for me in life, but in that moment, I felt as if I should turn the table and be the one to minister to this pastor and help him understand what abortion really is and what it does to people. I believe he was a good and caring man. I believe he heard my story and was filled with compassion for me. And he in no way condemned me or tried to put any legalistic yoke upon me. But he also didn't see my deepest need, nor did he know how to speak to it. For me to hear that I shouldn't be so hard on myself was like a man of God telling me that "the blood stain on your hands was really not that bad, and yes, you've been through something hard but you're young and you have your whole life in front of you, so don't fret; it's going to be okay."

So why didn't those words satisfy? What did I need to hear from that shepherd that day? I believe I simply needed to hear and be convinced of this: that the blood shed by the Lord Jesus Christ on the cross was sufficient to pay my debt and that His blood speaks louder than the blood of my children that cries out from the ground. It's that truth that will lift the yoke of bondage, set the captive free, and will breathe new life into a deflated soul.

Receiving that truth would not have been the end of my healing journey, but it certainly would have been a beginning. When those of us who were once abortion-wounded were able to lay hold of that foundational truth, then we could at least accept that God had pardoned us and that He had released us from our prison of guilt and shame. His grace and mercy take on a new reality for us when we experience its power and when we can see PAID IN FULL stamped over our certificate of debt.

Years later, after I'd experienced much healing and by God's grace gained the ability to minister to others, the Lord revealed that He still had more for me. I was discovering that there is always a fresh revelation that can bring another layer of healing that takes you deeper still.

I once confessed my abortion to a Catholic priest. It's not that I did not feel thoroughly forgiven and pardoned from the Lord, because I did, and it's not that I felt like I was still holding unforgiveness toward anyone, because I felt like all those relationships had been reconciled. Still, I felt the prompting of the Holy Spirit to confess my abortion to him. In response, he said several good things, but one phrase pierced my heart. He said, "Karen, as a representative and on behalf of the body of Christ, I declare that we forgive you." Try to imagine how that hit me. I know that the Bible teaches that we are members of one another and that when one suffers, we all suffer, but I had never considered or been in a context where I could ask the body of Christ to forgive me for how my sin affected them and our collective conscious. But the Lord sent me this priest to release a word of forgiveness to me on behalf of the family of God and the body of Christ. Now that was a morsel that satisfied my soul.

Wounded and Unable to Serve

So why do I use the term abortion-wounded church? Even though it's impossible to get statistics that tell the whole story, a recent study released by LifeWay Research in November 2015 (lifewayresearch.com) reveals that 70% of American women who have abortions identify themselves as Christian.[3] This includes broad definitions of Catholics, Protestants, Evangelical, Charismatic, Fundamentalist, and Non-Denominational. It is impossible to know the true faith of these women's hearts, but something in their lives makes them identify themselves as God-believing or as part of His Church. In my case, I was certainly one of those statistics. Even though these statistics cannot tell us everything we would like to know, they do reveal enough to be alarming.

That same study also revealed that 76% of those taking the survey said that local churches had no influence on their decision to abort.[4]

If you are a pastor, priest, clergy, chaplain, or lay leader, I hope these statistics are disturbing to you. How can these numbers be so high? Why is there seemingly so little differentiation between Christian and non-Christian American women and men choosing to abort their children? Why does the church have so little influence in our culture regarding life and death choices for unborn children? Where is the disconnect? My prayer is that these questions would cause you to wrestle not just with the *why* but would lead you to ask *what* does the Lord want me to do?

The struggle for the abortion-wounded parishioner is not just that they live with their own secret torment, but they avoid serving at church except in ways that are non- threatening. You see, it makes her anxious to be around children, so she can't serve in children's church. He or she can't help chaperone a youth group trip because he or she worries about what they'll do if students start asking about sex or one of them confesses to having an abortion. It's too risky to join a home fellowship group because participants might be asked to share their testimonies, and that is too vulnerable. When you're still in bondage to your abortion wounds, your plan is to stay silent, behave yourself, don't cause problems, and hope no one asks too many questions. A heart in that condition can only embrace your church's mission and vision intellectually and from the comfort of their back-row pew.

Spiritual Forces

Even though I had a core conviction that abortion was wrong and was taking the life of a baby, other influences and pressures were strong enough to cause me to consent to the thing I said I was against. I unpacked those things in my story in an earlier chapter, but let me emphasize at least two of the spiritual forces that make people vulnerable to abortion.

There are real spiritual forces that can feel more overpowering than your convictions and conscience. Fear is certainly one of them, and deception is the other. A spirit of fear will fuel a lie and make it global ("It will ruin my whole life"). It's non-specific and is always full of hopelessness. Deception, on the other hand, can sound reasonable, practical, and even wise ("I'm too young and immature to have a baby"). These influences don't require that you have faith in God or that you would need the help of others. In fact, you can get an abortion on your own, and no one else has to know or be involved.

As with all lies, they are just that—lies that will betray you. It's just like what the White Witch said to Edmund in *The Lion, The Witch, and The Wardrobe:* "I'm a witch, fool. A witch doesn't have to keep promises. All she has to do is make them."

When these spiritual forces of fear and deception are coupled with human pride and rebellion, they gain control to overpower your soul. As a shepherd and spiritual authority, you cannot make someone repent of their pride and rebellion, but you can at least address those strongholds in people's lives through your preaching, teaching, and counseling.

As a shepherd and spiritual authority over your flock, and in conjunction with your church leadership and intercessors, you can spiritually address spirits of fear and deception. You can pray to bind them up in the name of Jesus in order to mitigate their influence on your flock. You can also loose the blessing of the spirit of truth, peace, and a sound mind upon your congregation (Matthew 16:18–19). This spiritual weapon of warfare carries tremendous weight and power to clear the spiritual air around the individuals and families in your care.

There could be many families in your congregation dealing with a crisis pregnancy situation who are going to make decisions one way or another about the life of a baby, even if they don't plan on ever telling you. The 2015 study sited earlier by LifeWay Research revealed that 43% of women who have had an abortion were attending a Christian church once a month or more at the time of one of their abortions.[5]

If you are a pastor, my hope is that you will take encouragement in this: Your influence, both through your teachings and through the corporate intercession of your leadership, will make a difference in the decisions people make, even if it's without your knowledge. You and your leaders can create a safe environment for your lambs to be rescued from the thicket if you bring forth the hard truth about abortion and couple it with your shepherding heart of love, mercy, and grace.

At the completion of our Deeper Still retreats, we give our participants a letter addressed to their pastor. This letter describes the healing journey they have just been through in this retreat, and it invites their spiritual leader into their ongoing spiritual health and growth. This letter helps to break the ice between the participant and their pastor. It is also intended to help the pastor affirm this new season of healing, wholeness, and integration into the body. *I cannot overstate how significant a pastor's invitation and affirmation will be in this person's life as they find their place in the body.*

Here are a few examples from those who have trusted God enough to make an appointment with their pastor and bring him into their story.

Pat shares:

> At the end of the retreat, you handed us the letter to give to our pastor. I immediately cringed in fear. Throughout the following week, I wondered if I really dared to speak openly and honestly to my pastor. Our new pastor was only 28 years old and fresh into ministry. I wondered would he understand? Would he reject me? Would he place judgment on me?
>
> That next Sunday I handed him the letter with trembling hands and a crackling voice. "Don't read it now," I said. "Read it next week, and then we'll talk." My anxiety level increased throughout the week as I anticipated his response. When the day approached, I was a nervous wreck. My husband and I met in his office. I began telling him my story. At one point he just put his head on the desk and started to groan. The thought entered my mind that he was going to reprimand me—then what would I do? But just the opposite took place. Instead of rejection, judgment, or criticism, he responded with tears of joy. He shook his head and affirmed how

> richly God's mercy and grace had been poured out to us.
>
> Our church is composed of many people who are living with addictions, homelessness, and other life-wounding hidden issues. He asked us to be part of the leadership team that would reach out to those who were wounded and hopeless. We knew our transparency would be key in building that trust with others. My husband and I knew it was time to share our abortion-recovery story with a larger group. We spoke on SOHL Sunday (Sanctity of Human Life Sunday). In the past this had been a Sunday we would skip. It was too painful. This year we shared how God patiently waits to redeem us and bring us into full reconciliation and restoration. The response was overwhelming and far greater than we could have imagined. Many men and women confessed to their abortions and other devastating dark secrets. The next week we continued praising God and confessing sin with one another. The Holy Spirit broke through and did amazing healing because of the Deeper Still letter telling me to go meet with my pastor.

In Sue's experience, she shared with two different pastors, and there was quite a contrast between the two. The first was the senior pastor of a large church where she is a member. She described it as a positive experience.

Sue shares:

> He was genuine and interested in hearing my story. He made good eye contact and I did not feel rushed. However, he seemed a little perplexed, as if he wasn't really aware of this problem in the church, but it was as if he wasn't sure how he would handle it if it did come up. But still, he seemed appreciative of the time to hear from me and learn new insights.

In contrast though, she made an appointment with a former pastor from a church she used to attend in another state, while on vacation.

Sue shares:

> He sat and listened but seemed a little guarded. At one point, he interrupted me and said, "I hate to burst your bubble, but I've never counseled with anybody who's had an abortion." I assured him that he had but he just didn't know it. I briefly shared my story. He didn't have much to say after that. He's never brought it back up to me or asked me any questions. It was awkward and emotionally unsatisfying.

Abortion Fatigue

Let's take a deeper look into what has weakened the influence of the church regarding the sanctity of human life and what can be done to gain it back.

I think it's worth acknowledging that one of the reasons abortion has become part of the landscape of our culture is because it's not an obvious moral sin for many people. We as a people, a culture, and a church have become so dull of heart when it comes to our spiritual and moral sensibilities that we either can't discern the truth that abortion is the shedding of innocent human blood, or we don't think it matters that much to God. We have a spiritual condition the Bible calls hardness of heart. As a post-Christian culture, we do not fear God nor particularly care about what He thinks about things. We have a severe case of abortion fatigue.

We are so weary of hearing about abortion and talking about abortion that it has become like abortion white noise, and we've learned to tune it out. It reminds me of a nature phenomenon that happens every summer in East Tennessee. Every July the cicadas have a "coming out" party, and you can't avoid it—at least at first. They make this shrill, piercing vibrating noise. It's loud, distracting, and it reminds me of a sound track from an alien movie. When this constant chorus is new, it's deafening and hard to ignore. But after a few weeks, you develop an ability to tune it out. It becomes part of the sounds of summer and you learn to live with it.

I think we've learned to do the same thing with abortion. It has become the never-ending, numbing drone of our media culture. The whole discussion gets reduced to ten-second sound bites and three-minute talking points. It has become the background noise of the culture of death. With time, you adapt to it and accept it as part of the way it is. Tragically, the enterprises of media and academia have gained more authority to frame the abortion issue than the Lord's Church.

Once you become abortion weary, you look for other less controversial issues to champion. Not that God isn't impassioned about every issue that is morally egregious, but every moral transgression has its roots in the rejection of the sanctity, dignity, and protection of human life. The truth is we live in an abortion-weary world, and at some point, there's going to be an abortion-weary tipping point. We, the Church, are going to be tempted to give in and give ourselves over to the culture of death that is permeating our thinking and numbing our souls.

Several denominations already have either given up on addressing the issue or worse, some have joined the ranks of abortion advocates and have begun to perform blessing ceremonies at abortion clinics. I know of some churches who have established a fund to pay for abortions for those in need.

When I feel myself growing weary (and believe me I have those moments) there are at least two go-to verses for me.

> But they who wait for the Lord shall renew their strength; they shall mount up with wings like eagles; they shall run and not grow weary; they shall walk and not faint. (Isaiah 40:31)

> And let us not grow weary in doing good, for in due season we will reap, if we do not give up. (Galatians 6:9)

We've Got to Talk about It

Not only are we tired of hearing about abortion, but we don't want to talk about it either. In fact, we don't even like to say the word. Think about it for a minute. When you say the word *abortion*, how does it make you feel? Say it several times in a row. Is it a word you just don't want to say to people? I have a theory. I think even the word abortion has a built-in curse on it. The word itself leaves a bad taste in your mouth. It has an ick factor, and if we can avoid saying it, we will. We would rather use a more euphemistic word if we must refer to abortion.

But in contrast, consider the word *adoption*. Say it several times. How does it make you feel?

It's not a word you feel you need to mask. In fact, adoption has a life-affirming feel to it.

(I'm not suggesting that adoption is not painful or that it doesn't require healing too, because it does). But adoption is God's idea and intended to be a life-giving provision. When your kids ask you what the word *adoption* means, you don't mind saying the word or explaining what it means. But who wants to tell their kids about abortion when they ask what it means?

Until we muster the courage to say the word *abortion* and then clearly define what it is, we're going to let the conspiracy of silence speak louder than the painful truth behind abortion. And if church leadership is not talking about it, trust me, your people aren't going to talk about it either. The 2015 LifeWay Research study indicates that 52% of churchgoers who've had an abortion haven't told anyone in their church.[6]

Again, if I may speak to my brothers and sisters who are clergy. I fully acknowledge that you have a tough job. You want to speak the truth in love, but it's hard to know how to do that when, statistically speaking, maybe a third of the women and men in your congregations have been involved with abortion in one way or another. Because no matter how lovingly and grace-filled you try to address the subject of abortion, the truth is that many cannot hear it. People with abortion-wounded hearts have a grid of condemnation and shame, and everything they hear about abortion gets filtered through that grid. And trust me, they are squirming in their seats even if they appear unphased on the outside.

But here's my encouragement—please don't choose to avoid it because some may not yet receive your grace. You can expose that it's the strongholds of shame and condemnation that keep them bound and unable to confess their sin and receive redemption and healing. When we're wounded, we let those strongholds define how we hear the message of salvation, forgiveness, and deliverance. Sometimes just calling out the elephants in the room will cause those elephants to bow before the powerful name of Jesus Christ.

When you demonstrate that *abortion* is a word we will not cower to in this church and that this church is not only going to be a safe place to talk about abortion but a safe place to heal from abortion, then you are becoming a change agent. Next, ask your congregation to put away their own sense of taboo about talking about abortion and be committed to becoming a caring and healing community. These shifts will begin to change the atmosphere regarding abortion and the rules of the engagement.

A Theology of Life

For the church to turn the tide on the culture of death, we need to make the theology of the sanctity of human life part of our core doctrinal orthodoxy. The sanctity of human life should not be considered a fringe doctrine, or a specialized side issue you are obligated to address once a year on Sanctity of Human Life Sunday. We need to normalize it as part of basic Christian discipleship and service. This means the church needs to help us develop a mindset for the sanctity of human life. To value human lives is to value image bearers of God. We are the pinnacle of His creation. He died for us to have eternal life. He did not die a criminal's death on the cross for the endangered spotted owl in your forest (nothing against spotted owls, but they do not have the same status as image bearers of God).

Dear pastor, we sincerely need to hear from you—but not just you—we need to hear from your elders, those gatekeepers who guard the orthodoxy and doctrines of the church. When they weigh in, it matters. The sanctity of human life needs to be in your Sunday School curriculum. Because even though it's hard to imagine right now, in ten years some of your fourth graders are going to be getting girls pregnant, and those girls are going to be getting abortions. Even though they learned that Jesus came in the form of a baby wrapped in swaddling clothes, they missed that God sends all His children to earth through the womb of a woman, and that He declares this creation good. Are your youth pastors and your young adult pastors openly addressing the sanctity of human life and human sexuality?

Are these truths and teachings permeating every sphere of your church culture?

If your strategy has been to delegate your pro-life messaging to the few pro-lifers in your congregation, then it will always be viewed as a fringe ministry. A disturbing segmenting has developed in the Church over the years. You have your Christians, and then you have your pro-life Christians. This ought not to be. Some are particularly gifted for and specifically called to certain pro-life outreaches, but as far as how we identify ourselves, what we teach, our discipleship models, and the ways we serve and give our finances, we should be weaving an open and life-affirming culture within the entire fabric of our faith community.

If you as spiritual leaders embrace these things, then you will begin to see women and men start to come out of the closet and trust you for help. It will start with a few, but when they gain their healing, then they will get their heart back and then their voice back, and once they get their voice, they will be able to expose the truth behind abortion and the lies that keep people bound.

Consider these verses:

> I have told the glad news of deliverance in the great congregation; behold, I have not restrained my lips, as you know, O Lord. I have not hidden your deliverance within my heart; I have spoken of your faithfulness and your salvation; I have not concealed your steadfast love and your faithfulness from the great congregation.
> (Psalm 40:9–10)

I remember the first time I shared my abortion healing testimony in a church service. It was a huge milestone not only in the sense that it was good for my own soul, but I witnessed how the Lord used my restored voice and healed heart to encourage others that God can forgive, deliver, heal, and set captives free. My simple testimony of God's faithfulness started a chain reaction of others coming out of the dark and into the light.

In my case, that experience didn't start by me going to my pastor and asking him if I could share my testimony (although I would do that now). Back then, I was still too timid to initiate such a thing, but that pastor came to me. I had shared my story with him at an earlier time, and he could discern that I was healed enough that he could entrust my voice to his congregation. He took a step of faith, and I took a step of faith, and God honored it in a big way.

When captives get set free, it's not just that they have a powerful testimony to share, but it's also that they are free to begin to serve in the church from a new place of authenticity, peace, and joy. They can become useful vessels in the Lord's house and fruitful vines in His vineyard. But when their hearts are still bound by underlying guilt, shame, and grief, then much of their service is driven by performance and the need to prove something to you, God, themselves, and others.

The End-Time Bride

I am fully convinced and convicted that when abortion-wounded men and women who are Christ followers accept the Lord's invitation to go deeper still in their journey to healing and lasting freedom, then we will see an army arise. This army will be made up of mighty warriors who can advocate for the lives of unborn children. But at present, that segment of the Bride of Christ considers itself unfit for the end-time church adventure. She believes that the glorious end-time in-gathering of the saints yet to be saved will be the inheritance of more worthy Christians. But I am confident that this soon and coming Bridegroom is fiercely committed not only to her redemption, but He will do anything to gain her affections and trust. He is coming for a bride without spot or wrinkle, and He will rescue her from the vicious pimp that stole her away and then enslaved her.

When she regains her identity and gets her voice back, she will become empowered to take up the charge for those who can't speak for themselves. Right now, most of this army is like the living dead. This Bride needs shepherds who will recognize that she has been taken captive and enslaved by another master. She may be sitting in the pew every Sunday morning, and he may be serving as a Sunday morning greeter, but their sense of personal destiny and contribution in the things of God and His Kingdom are superficial.

Reach across the Denominational Aisle

We all know there is strength in numbers, and strength will grow if you initiate prayer and dialogue with other clergy in your sphere of influence. If you could share with other pastors how you've made headway in your congregation, perhaps it would give them the courage to take similar steps.

The bigger your city, the more abortion clinics you have, and therefore the more abortion-wounded you have in your city and in your churches. Would you put it on your calendar twice a year to meet some fellow clergymen outside one of the abortion clinics in town just to pray on-site? Corporate prayers from local shepherds who gather in agreement and repentance for the shedding of innocent blood on their land begins to shake the heavenlies and strikes fear into the principalities of murder and immorality over your cities. This is one way you can begin to take back the ground lost to the spirit of child sacrifice.

I was hosting a pastor's luncheon one time, and after our presentation, I asked if there were any questions or comments. We wanted to encourage these leaders in any way we could regarding their knowledge, influence, and strategies for developing a culture of life and healing in their churches or ministries. There were several seconds of silence, then finally one pastor spoke up and simply asked for one thing. He asked for even one other pastor to join him at least once when he prays in front of the Planned Parenthood across the street from his church. He said it's a lonely place to stand alone praying in front of a clinic of death.

Spiritual Warfare

I don't want to leave any impression that taking steps to turn the tide on the culture of death and developing a culture of life and healing in your church is going to be quick or without cost. In fact, it's going to be long, hard, and at great cost. The spiritual forces that fuel sexual immorality, child sacrifice, and the subsequent torment of the souls of those involved are some of the most viscous forces I've ever witnessed or encountered. You must seek God for His strategy, wisdom, power, and timing. But do not lose sight of this truth: greater is He who is in you than he who is in the world! Amen!

Deeper Still would have never gotten off the ground or flourished like it has if it weren't for the supernatural power and intervention of Jesus Christ, who is calling His church into this battle with Him. We have built this ministry on the sure foundation blocks that God revealed were necessary for walking in victory. We have been diligent to establish a culture of worship and intercession. We invest in our city by praying a blessing over it and its leaders. We pray a blessing over our city's churches; we honor and seek relational favor with them. We are diligent to preserve the unity within our teams, and we stay under the authority and protection of our board of directors and our individual spiritual shepherds. All these spiritual disciplines help maintain a huge and thick wall of Holy Spirit fire around us. We place ourselves in the shelter of the Most High, and we abide under the shadow of the Almighty. These are all magnificent provisions from the God of angel armies.

Encouragement to Pastors

It is not my intent to impose a man-made yoke on the Lord's Church or on His shepherds. You are a tremendous blessing and provision to the Church. But if the Lord has given me a voice for anything, it is for this issue. The effects of abortion and all its hellish tentacles and ripples will not be overcome if the Lord's Church will not get involved.

If you are a pastor or ministry leader who has an abortion-wounded heart, you won't have victory over the enemy's accusations unless you receive your own healing. The enemy will dog you and blackmail you for the rest of your life unless you stop running and turn around and face your accuser with the blood of the lamb and the word of your testimony. If you come into the light and model the journey to healing and freedom, then you will open the door for millions of abortion-wounded Christians to step into the light and trust Jesus for their redemption, salvation, deliverance, and healing.

If you are a pastor or ministry leader who has never been personally touched by abortion, please don't conclude that you have nothing to bring to this table. It is you the abortion-wounded fear the most. One word of rejection or condemnation from you can reinforce all the lies they ever believed about "the Church," and you will never see or hear from them again. We need to hear your heart that you do not view us as second-class or "no-class" Christians but that you, too, believe that the blood of Jesus is enough to set us free from sin and death.

The Church in every generation has had its defining battles to fight and its causes to champion. In this 21st century, the sanctity of human life is surely one of these defining issues. Will He find us faithful? Will you speak up for those who can't speak for themselves? Will you bind up the brokenhearted and proclaim liberty to the captives and freedom to those in prison? Will you give them beauty for ashes, oil of gladness for mourning, and the garments of praise instead of a spirit of fainting?

> Let us rejoice and exult and give Him the glory, for the marriage of the Lamb has come, and His Bride has made herself ready. (Revelation 19:7)

If we lock arms, together we can prepare this Bride for her Bridegroom.

Action Steps

Here's a summary of some action steps for those in church leadership that can begin to change the tide of silence and apathy within the Church:

- Develop a strategy for regularly teaching and preaching about the sanctity of human life and include it in your Sunday school curriculum.

- Cultivate a culture of worship and intercession so you can hear God's heart concerning the issue of abortion and His strategy for victory and healing.
- Address the spiritual forces of fear, condemnation, and deception.
- Create a safe environment for abortion to be discussed in productive and redemptive ways.
- Establish resources for healing abortion-wounded hearts.
- Remove the stigma of fear that would prevent someone from talking with you and confessing his or her sin.
- Reach across denominational lines to encourage and learn from other pastors; meet to pray and dialogue about establishing a culture of life and healing.
- Be willing to share your own journey and to receive deeper healing for yourself.
- Partner with at least one other pastor and go pray in front of an abortion clinic at least once a quarter and see what happens in your heart.

8

Mother's Day and Father's Day

Now, What Do We Do?

IS IT JUST ME, or have you noticed a shift in attitude and in the atmosphere on those once-cherished Sunday mornings when we celebrated our mothers and fathers on Mother's Day and Father's Day? Even though none of us had perfect parents, it still felt good and right to acknowledge and honor our mothers and fathers for all they sacrificed on our behalf.

But in recent years I've become more aware of an awkward feeling arising on Mother's Day and Father's Day that is similar to how people respond to Sanctity of Human Life Sunday. It's that feeling in the sanctuary, especially on Mother's Day, when you feel more dread in the room than celebration. There's almost a collective sigh of relief after the pastor makes the obligatory announcement and exhortation regarding the day and then moves on to the next announcement.

How did we get here? These days used to be pretty simple and straightforward. You would thank your mother or father (and always remember to call your mother) for all they do for you. You would take them out to eat, buy them a card, a gift, or another necktie, right? But now there are so many subsets of family brokenness, barrenness, and bitterness that even if you have had a wonderful family legacy of good and stable parents, it seems to provoke more grief and jealousy in the have-nots than celebration for the haves. Even our pastors don't know how to honor the good while navigating through all the painful pitfalls of possibly offending someone or stirring up painful memories and family skeletons in the congregants sitting out there in front of him.

Just to put it all out on the table, let's name some of these subsets that can make Mother's Day or Father's Day more dreaded than celebrated. There are the blended families made up of moms and dads and stepmoms and stepdads. There are single moms and single dads, and then there are foster children with temporary moms and dads. There are women and men who have placed their children for adoption and feel the loss, and there are men and women who have been adopted but still carry painful mystery about their birth mother and birth father. There are those who have never been able to have children, and then there are those who have had their children taken away from them. There are those who have lost children to sickness or accident, and there are those who have suffered loss through miscarriage. And in this day and age, there are those who have the means to create their baby in a petri dish, and there are those who would not have the means for such technology. There are those who are thrilled to be pregnant and celebrate their first Mother's Day while the baby is in utero, and then there are those who do not want to be pregnant again on this Mother's Day. There are those who are single and desperately want to be married and have children and who always feel marginalized on Mother's Day or Father's Day. Then there are those who have been raised in an orphanage and only know caretakers as parents. There are those mothers and fathers who, for whatever reasons, do not feel worthy of being honored as a parent because of how they've failed their children, so they too would just as soon pass over this day.

And then there are those who have had their children aborted—some with consent, some without consent. And in most of those cases, the rest of the family members sitting in the pew next to them have no knowledge of the pain, guilt, and loss they carry.

Whew! That's a lot of reasons to avoid church on those Sunday mornings. So what's a pastor, a church, and a Christian supposed to do with all this pain, guilt, shame, and loss that gets stirred up on Mother's Day and Father's Day?

I can remember my own feelings of inadequacy and unworthiness for the first couple years of my marriage when on Mother's Day they would ask all the mothers to stand. I was a new stepmom, but because I hadn't birthed children of my own, I felt disqualified and self-conscious and thought that if I did stand up, then I should somehow explain my situation to everyone to justify why I stood up. I can laugh about that now because, after having a few more years of step-mothering under my belt, I began to feel entitled, because I now had some war wounds to show for it. But I can certainly affirm that feeling of being a second-class mother on Mother's Day. It's not a good feeling.

We didn't get in this complicated quagmire overnight, but we can take heart that Jesus is the Master of writing a new story and starting a new legacy. I certainly don't pretend to have all the answers, but I've given a lot of thought to how we could begin to turn the tide on those Mother's Day and Father's Day elephants in the room and begin to redeem those days.

God the Father and the Father Mantle

Let's first start by considering that God the Father is one of the members of the Holy Trinity. He is first a father, and when we become one of His children, He became our Heavenly Father and we gained all the privileges of sonship. The Bible is full of descriptions and demonstrations of the tender care of our Heavenly Father. Here are just a few:

> Fear not, little flock, for it is your Father's good pleasure to give you the kingdom. (Luke 12:32)

> Do not be like them, for your Father knows what you need before you ask Him.
> (Matthew 6:8)

> Be merciful, even as your Father is merciful. (Luke 6:36)

> Blessed be the God and Father of our Lord Jesus Christ, the Father of mercies and the God of all comfort. (2 Corinthians 1:3)

> He will tend his flock like a shepherd; He will gather the lambs in His arms; He will carry them in His bosom, and gently lead those that are with young. (Isaiah 40:11)

> But when the fullness of time had come, God sent forth his Son, born of a woman, born under the law, to redeem those who were under the law, so that we might receive adoption as sons. And because you are sons, God has sent the Spirit of his Son into our hearts, crying "Abba! Father!" So you are no long a slave, but a son, and if a son, then an heir through God. (Galatians 4:4–7)

For anyone who has felt the pain of an absent, neglectful, or abusive earthly father, once you receive Father God as your Heavenly Father, the door has opened for you to be fathered by the perfect Father, who is able to restore all that was lacking in your father-starved heart.

It's also a stunning truth that we are made in the image of God. And, as such, Father God has instilled in us certain characteristics of His father's heart. For the sake of this discussion, however, I would like to focus on just one aspect of this phenomena. If you were born a man-child, then you were automatically imbued with the foundational building blocks—or let's call it the spiritual DNA—of your Heavenly Father. And, therefore, He has purposed that you would grow in the image and likeness of this "Father DNA." That Father DNA is not only meant to be stewarded in you, but it is also meant to be passed on and imparted to others. God intends for every person He has created to be "fathered," and even if we don't get that from our own earthly father, He has made other provisions. I believe every man of God carries the mandate to father, if not biologically then certainly spiritually.

One responsibility of the church is to teach, model, foster, and celebrate this "father DNA" in its sons. As described in an earlier chapter, at our Deeper Still retreats, we call the stewardship of this "fathering DNA" the "Father Mantle." As a part of our retreat, we pray for our male participants that their fathering hearts would be awakened, healed, and commissioned to father the "orphan spirit" that has robbed millions of people of their identity as beloved sons and daughters.

The Mother Mantle

The Bible also gives us some beautiful metaphors of how God manifests His heart through the design of a woman, and He calls her mother. It was a delightful revelation for me the day the Holy Spirit brought a certain scripture to my attention. In Genesis 3:20 it says, "Now the man called his wife's name Eve, because she was the mother of all the living." But it's not until Chapter 4 we read that Eve conceived her firstborn child, Cain. So Eve was given the title Mother before she ever bore her first child. The implications of this are quite radical. The spiritual DNA of mothering was given to the first woman, made in the image of God.

In the same way that all men are endowed with the stewardship of fathering, every woman has been graced with the foundational building blocks to mother. We refer to this as the "Mother Mantle." These building blocks must be nurtured and brought forth, but they are part of our design as women made in the image of God. Is it any wonder that part of the curse of the fall was that there would be enmity between Satan's offspring and the woman's offspring? Satan knows the power of a mothering heart, and he knows that if he can abort a mothering heart and steal the offspring of Eve, then he can raise generations of spiritual orphans who will reproduce after their own wounded kind.

Let's look at a few Scriptures regarding the godly character of a mothering heart:

> Rejoice with Jerusalem, and be glad for her, all you who love her rejoice with her in joy, all you who mourn over her; that you may nurse and be satisfied from her consoling breast; that you may drink deeply with delight from her glorious abundance. For thus say the Lord, Behold I will extend peace to her like a river, and the glory of the nations like an overflowing stream; and you shall nurse, you shall be carried upon her hip and bounced upon her knees. As one whom his mother comforts, so I will comfort you; you shall be comforted in Jerusalem.
> (Isaiah 66:10-13)

> O Jerusalem, Jerusalem, the city that kills the prophets and stones those who are sent to it! How often would I have gathered your children together as a hen gathers her brood under her wings, and you were not willing!
> (Matthew 23:37)

> Whenever a woman is in labor she has pain, because her hour has come; but when she gives birth to the child, she no longer remembers the anguish because of the joy that a child has been born into the world. (John 16:21)

> Sing, O barren one, who did not bear; break forth into singing and cry aloud, you who have not been in labor! For the children of the desolate one will be more than the children of her who is married, says the Lord. (Isaiah 54:1)
> But we were gentle among you, like a nursing mother taking care of her own children. (1 Thessalonians 2:7)

> He gives the barren woman a home, making her the joyous mother of children. Praise the Lord! (Psalm 113:9)

Bring Back the Celebration

If every child born of God, at the least, possesses the building blocks for mothering and fathering, then why not call that out, affirm it, and pray for its fruition? Instead of giving motherhood and fatherhood a narrow definition that can only be wholeheartedly celebrated by those who fall into the "most blessed" category, why not pray for and celebrate the gift and stewardship of mothering and fathering we all possess?

Here's a possible way to address Mother's Day and Father's Day in a church service:

Mother's Day Blessing

As the family of God, on this Mother's Day, we want to take some time out of our service today to honor and encourage the stewardship of mothering. We acknowledge that the celebration of this day can be joyful for some and painful for others. But whatever your gains or losses have been regarding your mothering, we are confident that, today, the Lord is ready and willing to pour out His grace for healing, encouragement, and affirmation on all our ladies here today, young and old.

Let's first acknowledge that God Himself designed the gift of motherhood. He sent His own Son into this world, born of a woman, knowing that for this child's physical, emotional, and spiritual development he would need an earthly mother. Even from this example alone, we see how deeply Father God values a mother.

We would like to pray a mother's blessing over every lady in the house today. Whether you have physically borne children or not, we want to honor your mothering heart and want to bless you as you mother those God brings into your life that need your mothering touch. We also want to include our single women, our young girls, and even our baby girls who will grow up to be mothers someday.

We would like to ask all the ladies among us today to stand so that we can pray this blessing over you.

Father God, thank you for creating your daughters to possess the heart of a mother and for giving them the ability to nurture life and to care for those you put in their path that need their mothering touch. Will you bless them to be fruitful and prosperous in all the ways that they mother? Will you give them wisdom and grace as they extend their mothering touch to others? For those who have experienced loss and hope deferred, will you bring them healing and encouragement? For those who are waiting and watching for your promises to be fulfilled give them peace and perseverance. And for our young who will be mothers someday, lead them in the way of righteousness and keep their hearts tender and teachable. Lord, we need godly mothers to raise the generations to come and to bring healing to the orphan's cry. We thank you, God, that you watch over your word to perform it and that you will do exceedingly abundantly beyond all we can ask or think. So we ask for these blessings in the mighty name of Jesus. Amen!

Father's Day Blessing

As the family of God, on this Father's Day, we want to take some time out of our service today to honor and encourage the stewardship of fathering. We acknowledge that the celebration of this day can be joyful for some and painful for others. But whatever your gains or losses have been regarding your fathering, we are confident that today the Lord is ready and willing to pour out His grace for healing, encouragement, and affirmation on all our men, young and old.

Let's first acknowledge that God Himself is a father and designed the gift of fatherhood. And He has given the stewardship of fathering to men. What an awesome privilege and responsibility! Father God entrusted Joseph to be Jesus's earthly father. Joseph probably had his moments of doubt, wondering if he was up to the task, but his simple "yes" and obedience was all that God required; God supplied the rest. This child, Jesus, also needed an earthly father for His physical, emotional, and spiritual development. Even from this example alone, we see how deeply Father God values a father.

We would like to pray a father's blessing over every man in the house today. Whether you have biological children or not, we want to honor your father's heart and bless you as you father those God brings into your life that need your fathering imprint. We also want to include our single men, our young boys, and even our baby boys in this blessing, for they too will grow up to be fathers someday.

We would like to ask all the men among us today to stand so that we can pray this blessing over you.

Father God thank you for creating your sons and endowing them with a father's heart. Thank you that, as image bearers, they too can cry out for a heart like Yours. Today, God, would you pour out your fathering spirit upon all your sons in this place, young and old? Will you expand their hearts and give them the capacity to embrace the stewardship of fathering? Give them courage, strength, vision, wisdom, leadership, and a servant's heart. Where they have been wounded, would you heal them so they can take up their swords and shields once again and fight for their families? Where they have failed, will you pour out your grace and forgiveness upon them and grant them a new beginning? Where they feel weak and weary, will You show them that You are the great I Am and that You can supply all their needs? Where they feel disqualified, will you show them that they have a place at your table and that you have great Kingdom exploits for them? Would you commission them to go out and find the lost sheep and run to meet the prodigal and to kill the fatted calf for every lost son that comes home? Father God, you hear the cry of the orphan, and You promise to be a father to the fatherless. Will you raise them up to hear the cries and answer the call? We ask for these blessings in the mighty name of Jesus. Amen!

New Wineskins for a New Day

In all of history, I don't know if it's ever been more important that we affirm the ministry of mothering and fathering than it is now. If we, the body of Christ, do not champion the cause of the orphan (whether physical, spiritual, born, or unborn) then raising our children will be left to other cultural or governmental institutions. Our children have the best chance to thrive when we heal, equip, and empower our men and women to take up their father and mother mantles.

Healing Exercise

To close out this chapter on blessing our mothers and fathers, I'm going to include a prayer that we pray during our Deeper Still retreats. It's a prayer for all the Church. It's a prayer of repentance for the iniquities of our ancestral mothers and fathers and for the iniquities that have been passed down through the generations. We're asking for the Lord's mercy on our generational lines.

Prayer of Repentance for Our Familial and Cultural Iniquities

Dear Lord, we realize that as a people, a culture, and a nation, we have willfully rebelled against your laws and the weight of our iniquities have defiled our families, our culture, and our land. We also acknowledge that the consequences of our iniquities can be visited upon our children.

We confess our familial, cultural, and national iniquities of:

- Rejecting you as creator
- Denying the sacred nature of human life
- Spilling innocent blood on our land
- Making choice and personal rights into a self-serving idol
- Defiling our bodies and minds with sexual immorality

Lord, we confess and repent on behalf of our ancestral family, church, city, state, and nation. Please forgive us of these transgressions and iniquities and heal our land.

Now, Lord, we stand before you as individuals, and we renounce our agreement and alliance with all of these cultural lies and strongholds. Would you sever all the tentacles that would keep our hearts, minds, bodies, or relationships in bondage to this worldly system?

Lord, we also acknowledge that our iniquities could result in a generational curse being passed onto our children and our children's children (Exodus 20:5). We repent for these iniquities. We acknowledge that your judgments are just and deserved, but our hope is in your word that assures us that Your mercy triumphs over judgment (James 2:13).

We now ask you to apply the atoning blood of Jesus Christ, your forgiveness, and your gracious mercy to our generational lines. We renounce these generational strongholds, and we pray that the curse may be broken off our children and our children's children. We claim back all the ground given up to Satan through our iniquity and the iniquity of our ancestors. We pray that our children can be forerunners in our family and in their generation for walking in righteousness and purity and that they will bring generational blessings to our family and our nation.

We now affirm and declare that:

- You are Creator God.
- Human beings are created in your image and should be honored as such.
- All our personal preferences and choices are under the authority of your holy Scripture and your Lordship in our lives.
- Our bodies are not our own, but we have been bought with a price and we will glorify you with our bodies (1 Corinthians 6:19–20).

Empower us to be ambassadors of your light and life in this dark and dying world.

In Jesus' name, Amen!

9

Awake, Awake, Awake

Locking Arms with Our Brothers

HE GOT TO HIS FEET during our prayer meeting, and with fresh conviction, passion, and authority, he announced, "Awake, Awake, Awake!"

We were gathered to pray about men and abortion. We were seeking the Lord and asking Him to move in the hearts of men around the world. This movement needs their leadership for sure, but the most important step before they can be effective leaders is that they too must submit to the surgeon's knife of the Great Physician and allow their hearts to be healed and set free from the ravages of abortion.

Their abortion-wounded hearts keep them from having a mindset for entering this battle in a redemptive and restorative way. Much ground has been lost, as our men and brothers have lost their sense of identity as men, fathers, protectors, providers, and leaders. We cannot turn the tide on our culture of death until our men lock arms with us women and together we begin to rebuild the ancient ruins. One of the promises God gives us when we say yes to His restoration plan is that "they shall build up the ancient ruins; they shall raise up the former devastations; they shall repair the ruined cities, the devastations of many generations" (Isaiah 61:4).

The abortion debate goes on and on, year after year, and rarely is it even considered that a man would—or should—have a legitimate voice in this debate. If a male politician, for example, speaks out to defend the life of the unborn, he is immediately jumped on, politically castrated, and accused of hating women. If men are not secure in their identity as leaders and protectors of the innocent, and if they don't have a clear understanding that they have been commissioned by their creator to fight for our families, then they will be paralyzed into passivity. If men take their identity cues from the angry, wounded (albeit well-intentioned from their worldview perspective) feminist voice of the culture, they will conclude that not only do they not have a right to enlist in this army, but it will be a lot safer for them to stay home and mind their own business.

Cassy Fiano, a writer who blogs at a website called *Abortion Gang*, expresses her feelings this way:

> I want to silence all the male voices in the abortion discussion. The main anti-choice voices for the US are also all men. In fact, the majority of persons in government who are anti-choice, are men. . . . And so I want to silence the voices of all men. I am so tired of men giving their opinion about abortion. I am so tired of it that I am willing to sacrifice the voices of all the men who support women. I truly believe that if men were no longer allowed to speak on the topic of abortion, every country would be pro-choice.

Wow! Really? Let's think about the implications of that sweeping statement. Even if we set aside our basic right of freedom of speech in this country, if the basic biological facts are that every human being is made up of 23 chromosomes from the male and 23 chromosomes from the female, then how can someone assert that a man who was a co-creator with a woman should have no voice, no interest, no heart, or no vote concerning the child they co-conceived? I'm not addressing the issue of if every man who has ever fathered a child is worthy of being a father any more than is every woman who ever gets pregnant worthy of being a mother, but you can't, across the board, remove men from the equation of the preservation and welfare of human life any more than you can remove women from the equation. Let it sink in for a minute that every aborted baby has a mother and a father.

I guess if a man is pelted with certain emasculating slogans long enough, he eventually allows these defining accusations to sink into his heart and mind until he believes them himself. After a while, all his sensibilities for why he would fight for the lives and well-being of women and children in the first place have been so re-programmed that he finds himself pelting those same slogans to other men in an eerie self-fulfilling-prophecy. The next thing you know, this warrior becomes a peacekeeper whose redefined mission is to keep quiet, avoid the land mines, and look for another kind of battle to give his heart to—all while his offspring are being killed off right before him. His last victim-like rationalization for laying down his sword goes something like this: *Besides, who am I to talk ... if people knew my past, I wouldn't have any credibility anyway.*

Here's a contrast for you: My brothers, in the Kingdom of God, your life can be redeemed from your past. God will pick you up, turn you around, and put His robe of righteousness on you. He will clothe you in garments of salvation, He will place His sonship ring on your finger, He will kill the fatted calf in celebration of your new heart, and then He will send you out to be a force for redemption, restitution, and restoration. It's only in Satan's kingdom that you will always be known as a permanent hypocrite and loser. Which kingdom do you want to live for?

How did we get here? How have our Warriors lost sight of their mission? What makes a man lay down his sword and retreat in confusion and fear from a battle that should be second nature to him? I wonder if part of the answer lies in the confusion about whom or what we're really fighting.

Imagine this scenario with me. Back in the day when a mom sent her children off to school, to play, or to run an errand, the older or bigger brothers were commissioned to look after and protect their sisters, right? Then as those boys grew older, they began to take a greater interest in girls beyond just their sisters, and they developed a built-in conviction and desire to fight for all damsels in distress. In addition, those same young men were also taught to respect and not talk back to their mother, grandmother, or teachers.

How confusing it must be when one day those same men find themselves on the battlefield of life, whether it's professionally, socially, politically, in a college classroom, or even in a church Sunday school class and they discover that on the other end of his "I protect, defend, and show respect to women and children" sword is a woman that looks a lot like those he's been programmed to protect all his life, but she also has a sword and it's aimed at his heart. It's not a sword to protect our unity—it's a sword that draws the battle lines. What is he supposed to do? What are his choices?

In his mind, he's not sure how to separate the mission of protecting the life and well-being of women and children from the female who stands before him with claws out and insisting that he doesn't have a dog in this fight. If she confronts or challenges his position (even if her debate tactics include barbs and sarcasm), it is generally viewed as fair game. If, on the other hand, that man confronts or challenges her position, it is viewed as an attack or worse. But the underlying assumption seems to be that men, in general, are too clueless or obtuse to understand what would be a benevolent solution for women and children in crisis—*so stay out of it!*

Now I know that might seem a little harsh and overgeneralized, but these are the attitudes that get press time. These are the attitudes that I believe cause men to lay down their swords and retreat from the bigger-picture battle of defending the life of our unborn children, making provision for their mothers, and working to strengthen our nuclear families.

For Christ followers, we know that the real enemy is first spiritual. We know that we fight forces that are not flesh and blood but are spiritual powers and principalities in heavenly places. We also fight sin in the heart and mind, which all amounts to enmity between the sexes.

I recently heard a metaphor that sounded fresh and hopeful to me. If women are pink and men are blue, what do you get when you mix pink and blue? You get purple. Purple is one of those colors of God. It reflects His rich beauty, strength, and royalty. It also reveals the royal standing of those of us who are His sons and daughters. I think there's great hope for a battle strategy that entails enlisting the best of the feminine heart with the best of the masculine heart. Then we can identify the real enemy, clarify our mission, and gain back the ground we've lost. Only then will the army of God be complete and equipped to defeat the spirit of child sacrifice as it manifests itself in our day and age. Together we can work to heal the ravages of those with blood on their hands, and those who have abortion-wounded hearts.

I love the story of Judge Deborah in the Old Testament (yes, there was Judge Deborah long before the reality TV shows). The Lord raised up Deborah, a prophetess, as a judge in Israel. The Bible records in the story of Deborah that, first of all, she summoned Barak to battle. "Has not the Lord, the God of Israel, commanded you 'Go gather your men at Mount Tabor, taking 10,000 from the people of Naphtali and Zebulun. And I will draw out Sisera, the General of Jabin's army." Jabin was the King of the Canaanites and the enemy of Israel.

Barak said to her, "If you will go with me, I will go, but if you will not go with me, I will not go." She said, "I will surely go with you ..." When the time was right, Deborah said to Barak, "Up! For this is the day in which the Lord has given Sisera into your hand. Does not the Lord go out before you?" In their combined leadership, they defeated the army of Sisera.

As women, and especially those of us who have received healing from our abortion-wounded hearts, we have gotten our voices back and we have had our hearts set free. We have done the work of repenting for having our children sacrificed and we have forgiven those men who have wounded our hearts. As a result, we have come to recognize the strength of our brothers and that they are not the enemy. We can now summon them to take up the sword for the cause of life ... *and surely we will go with you!*

Back to that prayer meeting I referred to at the beginning of this chapter, the rest of the word the Lord gave our friend Wayne went like this, "There is a deep sleep sitting over the men, a deep slumber, a stupor. They are awake enough to function, but not awake enough to enjoy life." The Lord is standing in front of His throne and has proclaimed, 'Awake, Awake, Awake' to the men of the earth. He has given orders to His messengers to proclaim this word to the ends of the earth. It's the preaching of the gospel and the word of freedom that will shake them out of their slumber."

What Happened When We Started Inviting Men to Our Retreats?

Surprised, apprehensive, fearful, too risky—these were some of my thoughts and feelings when I first sensed the Lord telling me it was time to invite His sons to the Deeper Still retreats. He had been planting these seeds in my heart for years, but I always dismissed them as, "That can't be God." But right from the beginning when we first started doing Deeper Still retreats for women, inevitably, one of the participants would say, "Do you have something like this for my husband?" or "I wish I could send my boyfriend to this retreat." My response was usually, "I know they need healing too, but God's going to have to raise up someone else to do that."

I felt like I was just beginning to understand how to minister to women, and I figured that to add men into the mix would be risky, at best. After all, part of the issue for women is an inability to trust men because they have been wounded by men. Then there's the issue of how group dynamics change when you mix men and women together. But probably my biggest concern was the emotional and spiritual vulnerabilities that can come into play when wounded women and wounded men are on a similar journey. It is likely that some have not yet learned healthy social boundaries or have not yet closed the dark spiritual doors that have caused them to operate in seductive ways (that they may not even aware of) when around the opposite sex.

But here's the good news: when you trust God and obey His leading, timing, and wisdom, He will guard and protect that which you have entrusted to Him. As we made it a non-negotiable to honor God's presence and simply join Jesus in His healing work in the lives of these women and men, then His power would be released in the most awesome ways. The Holy Spirit would soften the hardest heart, enable forgiveness to flow, and those you thought were wounded beyond repair would allow new hope to spring up from the inside out. Right before our eyes, we witnessed that thick wall of enmity, judgment, and bitterness between the sexes come tumbling down.

Here are a few comments from men and women who shared a retreat together.

Samantha shares:

> As I was able to see each of you men sharing your pain, your stories, your fear, all of that helped me to see that your suffering was as real as mine. I want to ask for forgiveness from you men, because in my fear, I have hurt many of you as well. Please forgive me for thinking you were not

trustworthy, not worthy of respect and appreciation. But I am thankful that it is not too late for me. I look forward to how the Lord will redeem this area in my life as well.

Beth shares:

I am incredibly grateful to the men for giving me the words to help [my husband] know that he is not alone and that it is his pain too not just mine.

Samantha shares:

God used two groups of men to radically change my heart toward men. I'm used to associating manly strength with intimidation and fear. The first group was the team members. Even though some of the men were a little physically imposing, there was a gentleness that shone through their eyes and in the way that they carried themselves that took my breath away. They felt safe, which was something I had never really experienced before. The second group was the men participants who were on the retreat. I saw God transform them from the men who just looked broken and defeated to warriors who God has called to protect and defend. All in all, God gave me a vision of what He is like through all of these wonderful men I met. In them, I saw the fierce gentleness of God along with the protective strength of a loving father. I cannot say that all of my wounds are gone, but something in my heart

> has dramatically changed regarding men and it has given me great hope.

Keith shares:

> And thank you to all the ladies for welcoming us men into your 'personal space.' Sharing your pain allows us to realize how deeply wounding our actions toward you have been. God is using your testimony for His glory in helping to awaken us men to our responsibility in abortion.

Angela's Story

Let me tell you about a precious sister named Angela who attended our retreat several years ago. I will never forget the impact of hearing her story, and I will never forget the awesome ways God met her that weekend. Let me share how the Lord used the men in our retreat to bring healing to Angela's heart regarding men.

From the age of 17, Angela had been raped five different times at the hands of men, most of whom she should have been able to trust. She also had two abortions. By the time we met Angela, she had come to know the Lord as her Savior and was growing in her relationship with Him.

In the retreat registration confirmation letter we send our women participants, we tell them that there will be men attending this retreat as well. Some women don't even hesitate at the thought of sharing a retreat with men, but other women like Angela have so much more at stake, especially when the subject is as sensitive as abortion and sexual sins and soul ties. The only time during our retreat that men and women participants are together is during large group teaching times and for meals. All the times of personal prayer ministry and telling their story is done in small groups or one on one with women ministering to women and men to men.

In her own words, Angela describes what she was experiencing when she first arrived at the retreat and was getting settled in:

> I noticed other people arriving and to my consternation, I kept seeing more and more men in the group. Suddenly, I started to get nervous, asking God what He was doing and what were all those men doing here? I prayed "God, you know how much I hate men. Why are You doing this to me?"

After hearing Angela's story that first night, I was just heartsick for her. As a team, we had already prayed long and hard for Angela, but we knew it would take a supernatural intervention of God to help her release all that pain and death into His capable nail-scarred hands.

I first saw her heart begin to let down some defenses as a few of our men team members shared some of their stories of being healed from abortion. The men that serve on our team are stellar men indeed. They are honest, humble, kindhearted, and so honoring of the sisters that attend our retreats. I knew these brothers would hold a key to some of Angela's healing.

During the Saturday afternoon session on breaking unholy soul ties (inappropriate bonds), two of our women team members led Angela through those prayers. In Angela's words:

> I had still been carrying the baggage of all the men who took pieces of my heart and soul, and my heart had many holes that I wanted filled with God's love and tenderness. I didn't think it was possible ever to get this back but slowly, during that session, I began to have a heart for the men who hurt me. . . . I prayed for them and forgave them for the wrong they had done to me. After releasing all the bondage and soul ties, I felt free. I felt like I could breathe again, and I felt a hundred pounds lighter.

On Saturday evening, after a full day of healing and breakthrough for everyone, we give an opportunity for our participants to share with everyone how God had ministered to them that day. This is the first time that the men hear some snippets of the women's stories and vice versa. It is during this time that we see the hearts of our men broken and filled with compassion for what these women have endured. One of the comments we often hear from our men after those times of sharing is "I had no idea how much we hurt you."

Angela shared a little of her story and how the Lord had given her the supernatural grace she needed to forgive the men who violated her so cruelly. It was so beautiful to see this new, emerging story that God was weaving in Angela's heart all weekend.

One of the things we find ourselves saying a lot at our retreats is, "It's not over until it's over!" We might say our final Amen—but it's not over until the Lord says His final Amen! We had just finished up our Sunday morning brunch, which is our last official event of the retreat. But as I was saying our final goodbyes and our *shalom* and preparing to go home, Angela came up to me and asked if she could share something.

In Angela's words:

> I asked Karen if I could address the men on this retreat. I want to say that I am sorry for the way I've thought about you and treated you, and not just you but men in general. The day I walked in, I didn't know why God had brought me here with all you men. This morning, though, I was awakened again, and God instructed me that I needed to apologize to the men here and publicly forgive all the five men that had raped me. I ask you (as representatives of men in general) for your forgiveness for the agony and hurt I caused you.

Next, on their own initiative, our men team members went into action. Bruce motioned and asked all the men to surround Angela in a circle. Then we women surrounded the men. In Angela's words:

> The next thing I knew, I was in the middle of all these men who were forgiving me, and at the same time, I was not feeling violated. It was as if God was saying, "You're safe now." They all hugged me, forgave me, and told me they loved me, their new sister. At this, my heart melted. I

> really didn't feel uncomfortable for the first time in my life. I forgave them and they forgave me. It was a remarkable feeling.

Right after that, one of our male participants, Keith, asked me if he could share something. He had shared how the Lord had broken his heart for the way that men had so often run over or violated the hearts of His daughters. And that as a man and as a representative of a brother in Christ, he wanted to express his heart and God's heart toward them. This is the letter that Keith had written the night before. He sobbed as he read it. In fact, we all sobbed. There wasn't one woman in the room, including us (and the kitchen staff) that didn't receive a healing from the words that this man of God spoke into our hearts that day.

Keith's Letter

> Ladies,
>
> No men got together and voted for me to represent them to you, so I am saying this on my own.
>
> But, I don't think I am alone in the words and feelings in this message to you.
>
> For all the times that men have used you, abused you, abandoned you, lied to you,
>
> Failed to stand, support, protect, serve, and lead you.
>
> For the cowardice, weakness, denial, selfishness, withdrawal, anger, blame, lack of spiritual grounding, and guidance.

For the times we pressured you for sex, caused you physical, emotional, and spiritual pain,

For not having the self-control to honor, respect, and cherish you, your virginity, your purity, your beauty, your worth.

For when you have been alone, with the black lion stalking you

And we ran away instead of roaring and running forward to protect you. For all the joy, dancing, and worship that you deserved to be joined in with but your partner refused.

For all these things and more, we were wrong! I am sorry. Please forgive us.

When he spoke these words, we could all feel the presence of the Lord so strong in the room. I knew that Jesus was so proud of this brother that just wielded the most powerful weapon of warfare in the spirit realm. His humble and honoring spirit coupled with his sincere confession and repentance had the power to demolish strongholds of bitterness and unforgiveness that have plagued many women for years.

Here's the point I want to make about Angela's story. Our women team members ministered beautifully to Angela that weekend as only sisters in Christ can. But what Angela received through our brothers that weekend, we women could not have come close to touching. There is something in the godly masculine heart that the feminine heart needs to hear and receive in order for her soul to be healed and to be able to trust God's men.

Dear brothers, we can do this thing together. We need your strength, we need your courage, we need your tenderness, we need your leadership, and we need your voice.

And, surely, we will go with you!

Action Steps

Will you pray for the hearts of men to be awakened? Pray they will seek healing, that the walls of offense between men and women will be brought down, and that men and women will lock arms in this battle for life and healing.

10

Our Abortion-Wounded World

THIS BOOK WOULD not be complete if I did not shed some light on the scourge of abortion on a worldwide scale. The United States accounts for fewer than 2% of the world's annual abortions. Internationally, statistics reveal anywhere from 42 to 56 million abortions occur every year.[7] As mind numbing as those numbers are, we can't just ignore them as if that reality is someone else's problem.

If what I've described in this book and the testimonies I've shared are a microcosm of what's going on in the hearts, minds, and lives of billions of people around the world every day of every year, then we have a huge global crisis. The truth is we live in an abortion-wounded world. It's a deadly blight on the peoples and the nations of the earth, but this affliction is a hidden one. Whether someone chose an abortion or an abortion was forced upon them, no one wants to go public with their inner torment. This affliction is not recognized as a crisis in our world like starvation, disease, or even sex trafficking, but it is every bit as deadly to the soul and the spirit of the nations.

Deeper Still has had opportunities to minister in some international settings, and our materials have been used in many others. As we have led international people through our healing retreat, it has been such a wonderful and humbling experience to see how the Word of God, the Holy Spirit, and the body of Christ are able to transcend cultural and language barriers. We have had participants from Africa, South America, Eastern Europe, and China. We have a lot to learn from each other, but we observed early on that we all shed the same tears over our sorrows. We all need the same Savior.

LIFE International is a wonderful ministry that has directly taken the message and theology of the sanctity of human life into 64 nations and has influence and materials in close to 90 nations, www.LIFEInternational.com. Praise God for this pioneering movement to reach the other 98% of the abortion-vulnerable world. In recent years, LIFE International has used a version of our Deeper Still materials as part of their abortion healing training in 29 countries. They, too, have witnessed firsthand that although people come from different cultures, traditions, and worldviews, certain things are universal and cripple people the world over. These are things like guilt, shame, grief, regret, fear, anger, and hopelessness.

The abortion-wounded heart is found in every tongue and tribe, and many of those people have no knowledge of a God who would have great compassion on them if they would just call upon His name. He wants to heal them and free them from the shackles that have them bound. But He also wants to renew their minds with the truth that their offspring are heaven sent and should be considered their most treasured resource and inheritance.

Deeper Still is now offering retreats specifically for Chinese women and men. Those who come from mainland

China have a much different cultural landscape than we do in the United States. They live in a governing culture that denies the sacredness of human life and that people are created in the image of God. A worldview devoid of that fundamental truth will treat its people differently. Instead of being valued intrinsically, the question is are you an asset or a liability to our society?

As our Chinese sisters and brothers have shared their stories, we have become painfully sensitized to the "yokes of man" that these precious sisters and brothers have lived under, including forced abortions. Many Chinese women, right from their birth, are viewed as a disappointment to their family because they were girls. One of our Chinese sisters had lived most of her life trying to achieve success in a way that would please her father like he would be pleased if she were a son. Her abortions were motivated by a culture of performance, family success, and personal gain. We were so grateful the Lord made a way for her to come halfway around the world to hear the truth about how her Heavenly Father views her. And you can imagine how beautiful and joyous it was for us to witness that yoke being lifted off her as she progressed through the weekend. Women such as these are a "first fruits" representation for the healing of an abortion-wounded nation.

One of the spiritual challenges for Chinese women and men who are abortion-wounded is that they have little or no theological knowledge of what the Bible teaches regarding the value of human life. They are clearly living with all the torment of guilt, shame, and grief typical of abortion wounds, but they have no conviction that it was their abortions that brought this bondage upon them. The appeal from our Chinese sisters and brothers is this: "Help the Chinese

Church receive the truth about the sanctity of human life. Then we can begin to recognize our need for repentance and healing."

The testimony of so many abortion-wounded people is this: "it affected every area of my life." If you think about all the women and men in the world who have participated in abortion, and if they, too, are living with these consequences in every area of their lives, then addressing their abortion-wounded heart could revolutionize their lives, not to mention their nation.

Think this through with me for a minute. If you do a scriptural study on the consequences and judgments for breaking God's commandments—including the shedding of innocent blood on a nation or on its people—it's not a pretty picture. Bloodguiltiness will unleash all kinds of curses on nations and their people. These include things like drought, famine, wastelands, barrenness, disease, hardness of heart, captivity, etc. (Joel 3:19, Isaiah 59:7, Psalm 106:38, Jeremiah 7:30–35, 19:4–15, 2 Kings 24:3–4, Deuteronomy 28:15–68). If we couple that reality with the familial curses that our individual iniquities can release into our family generational lines, then we can see why our world is in a constant state of crisis in one way or another (Exodus 20:5, Ezekiel 18:30–32).

If these things are true, then doesn't it stand to reason that much of our efforts to bring humanitarian aid and justice ministries to the nations of the world are addressing the symptoms rather than the root cause? If much of our humanitarian and environmental problems are physical consequences of breaking God's spiritual laws, i.e., shedding of innocent blood, idolatry, immorality, etc., then why aren't we Christians focusing more on the spiritual problems of the world—starting with the Church itself? I am not trying to criticize humanitarian intervention—it's a way to bring God's mercy and grace to a needy world, and it's a witness of God's existence and His love. But I am trying to shed light on a deeper cause of these crises.

The blood of the innocents is crying out from the land. Who can hear it? When will they get justice? How is the worldwide Church addressing the blood-drenched lands of the nations?

I don't want to oversimplify these issues too much, but consider this: What if it was part of the strategic ministry plan for every missionary organization and every church planter to not only plant churches for the sake of getting the gospel into foreign lands and for getting people saved, but, in addition, as part of their core discipleship strategy, they would teach people the theology of the sanctity of human life? When people have knowledge of biblical truths, then the Holy Spirit can begin to work. When the Holy Spirit is given access to people's hearts and begins to renew their minds, then they begin to get convicted about the spiritual strongholds and idols that have held them captive.

Healing the Land

At the beginning of this book, I shared about my own abortion story and my journey to healing and wholeness. One aspect of that journey was to return to the city where I had my abortion, which was in Pittsburgh, Pennsylvania, and to repent on the land for my part in shedding innocent blood in that city.

When a city allows abortion to be part of its commerce, then the people of that city are partnering with a spirit of murder and violence. That kind of dark spiritual partnership can lead to all kinds of other strongholds such as sexual immorality, drug addiction, greed, and corruption. These dark spiritual strongholds impact the spiritual climate of a city. It can be difficult for the gospel to penetrate or be received in cities or regions where spiritual blindness, deafness, and unbelief have taken root.

When land is defiled by the shedding of innocent blood, God's righteous judgment will rest on the land, and it can become subject to certain curses and the influence of evil spirits. The good news is that the land can be cleansed and God's righteous judgments removed. If there is repentance for the sins committed on the land, then mercy and forgiveness can be extended and the curses and judgments against the land can be removed. This is possible because of the shed blood of Jesus Christ on the cross.

> If my people who are called by my name humble themselves and pray and seek my face and turn from their wicked ways, then I will hear from heaven, will forgive their sin and will heal their land. (2 Chronicles 7:14)

This was a huge revelation that I never even conceived of before the Holy Spirit taught me these spiritual truths and then convicted me to go do something about it. I can testify that after I did that act of repentance, not only did I experience more freedom in my own heart, but I knew I now had the spiritual authority to pray for the healing and spiritual revival of Pittsburgh.

Since that experience, I've made this principle a part of our Deeper Still retreats. We encourage all our participants to go back to the cities where they had their abortions and repent on the land and then bless that city with spiritual blessings.

Imagine with me what would happen if even a remnant of God's people from every nation, who have participated in the shedding of innocent blood through abortion or infanticide, went back to the cities where those abortions took place and repented on the land and released a blessing instead of a curse. What awesome things God could then do in those cities. If happened in the United States, I am confident we would see the stronghold of abortion come tumbling down like Jericho. If that happened with God's people in the nations around the world, I believe we would begin to see unprecedented openness to the gospel and God releasing and healing the nations.

This kind of action takes us beyond your own personal healing and into contributing to the spiritual health of your city, state, and nation. You can plant spiritual flowers in barren fields.

Healing Exercise: Prayer of Repentance to Cleanse and Heal the Land

This is a prayer you can take with you to the place where you had your abortion(s) so you can pray on location. If you can't get to the exact place, you can go somewhere in the city, state, or nation that would be representative of a governmental or spiritual covering or authority. For example, a capital building, court building, a church, etc.

Dear Lord,

I come before you today, along with these friends as my witnesses, to do my part in bringing your redemption and healing to this land. Lord, I repent for the part I played in the shedding of innocent blood on this land by aborting my child(ren).

I thank you that the shed blood of your Son, Jesus Christ, speaks louder than the blood that cries out from the ground (Hebrews 12:24). I ask you to apply the precious blood of Jesus Christ to this land and to cleanse it from all unrighteousness and defilement. By your mercy and grace, I ask you to remove your righteous judgment from this land, and any curses that have been on this land, as a result of my abortion(s) and set this land free from the curse of sin and death. I claim back the ground that was surrendered to Satan's kingdom because of my abortion(s).

I repent of and renounce any alignment or agreement I entered into with a spirit of death, murder, idolatry, violence, or immorality over this city and state. I completely fall out of agreement with any stronghold that has held this land and its spiritual atmosphere in captivity.

I also ask you to sever any unholy soul ties or attachment that was formed between me and this place and any evil entities connected to it. Will you sever it now by the sword of your Spirit?

Will you return to me any part of my soul that has been held captive by this place?

Lord, I now claim your Word that says, "If My people who are called by My name will humble themselves and pray and seek My face and turn from their wicked ways, then I will hear from heaven, will forgive their sin, and will heal their land" (2 Chronicles 7:14).

I now ask You, Lord, to heal and restore this land, that it might be used for your glory and that the purposes of your Kingdom will come to bear on this land, this city, and this state. Will you raise up a healing ministry in this city that will provide a fountain of life for those women and men who have been wounded and hardened by abortion? Let salvation come to many souls.

And Lord, I also speak forgiveness to those who performed or assisted in my abortion(s). Would You draw them by Your love and bring them to repentance and salvation in You, that they may know the power of Your blood and the freedom of Your grace and forgiveness?

Where there has been spiritual barrenness in this city and in this country, would You plant flowers so that Your beauty and restoration can be seen throughout this land? I bless this land, I bless this city, I bless this state, and I bless this nation in the name of Jesus Christ. Amen!

11

Justice and Mercy

HAVE YOU EVER wondered how it is possible that both justice and mercy and love and wrath can perfectly coexist in God? Unless you know God and His Word, you may not know that God is, in fact, perfectly just and righteous in His judgments but also wholly merciful, kind, and tenderhearted in His love. From our finite and sin-tainted human perspective, this truth creates an uncomfortable dissonance for us.

We would prefer that God would be either one extreme or the other. Then we could feel more justified in either loving Him or rejecting Him. But because He is perfectly both, we're forced into either a love/hate perspective of Him or we're simply challenged to surrender and embrace this truth about who He is. Even though we don't understand His ways, we can trust His motives. We can rejoice in the fact that the God of the universe operates in complete integrity and is congruent with His revealed character that is perfectly trustworthy and good.

> Righteousness and justice are the foundation of your throne; steadfast love and faithfulness go before you. (Psalm 89:14)

> For my thoughts are not your thoughts, neither are your ways my ways, declares the Lord. For as

> the heavens are higher than the earth, so are my ways higher than your ways and my thoughts than your thoughts. (Isaiah 55:7–9)

If you've ever been the victim of injustice, you love the idea that there is a God out there who is full of justice and that He will settle His accounts one day and you will finally be vindicated. On the other hand, if you were the perpetrator of injustice, you are more than grateful when the mercy of God has been graciously decreed from the courtroom of heaven and you are pardoned because He took the penalty you deserved.

Unless we embrace the whole of who God is in His justice and in His mercy, we will not be able to stand in faith regarding His goodness, righteousness, and love when His judgment and wrath are being poured out over the earth for the sins of people. We will be tempted to be offended by God's wrath and will end up cursing Him like the unbelievers.

The following are some of the most sobering and terrifying Scriptures in the Bible:

> The great day of the Lord is near, near and hastening fast; the sound of the day of the Lord is bitter; and mighty man cries aloud there. A day of wrath is that day, a day of distress and anguish, a day of ruin and devastation, a day of darkness and gloom, a day of clouds and thick darkness, a day of trumpet blast and battle cry against the fortified cities and against the lofty battlements. I will bring distress on mankind, so that they shall walk like the blind, because they

> have sinned against the Lord; their blood shall be poured out like dust and their flesh like dung. Neither their silver nor their gold shall be able to deliver them on the day of the wrath of the Lord. In the fire of his jealousy, all the earth shall be consumed; for a full and sudden end he will make of all the inhabitants of the earth.
> (Zephaniah 1:14–18)

And the same God made sure these words were also written into His eternal Word.

> Seek the Lord while he may be found; call upon him while he is near; Let the wicked forsake his way, and the unrighteous man his thoughts; let him return to the Lord, that he may have compassion on him, and to our God, for he will abundantly pardon. (Isaiah. 55:6–7)

> I have loved you with an everlasting love; therefore, I have continued my faithfulness to you. (Jeremiah 31:3)

> The steadfast love of the Lord never ceases; his mercies never come to an end; they are new every morning; great is your faithfulness.
> (Lamentations 3:22–23)

> Bless the Lord, O my soul, and forget not all his benefits, who forgives all your iniquity, who heals all your diseases, who redeems your life from the pit, who crowns you with steadfast love

> and mercy, who satisfies you with good so that your youth is renewed like the eagle's. The Lord works righteousness and justice for all who are oppressed. (Psalm 103:2–6)

As I shared in the introduction to this book, I have spent much time on the Big Island of Hawaii. Many spiritual parallels have been revealed to me through the natural beauty of this enchanting island. My husband and I follow a regular path on our morning walks down to the shoreline and around the beach. Most of the time, this is a serene walk. It's almost predictable. The sun comes up and it's perfectly warming but not scorching. The breeze is gentle, refreshing, and carries the smell of the ocean on its wings. The fronds of the palm trees dance as if to worship the King with Hosannas. The birds are singing, the fish are jumping, the geckos are darting, and all is right with the universe. It's easy to sense the peace, favor, and pleasure of God in that place.

One morning, though, I had a completely different experience on my predictable walk. Apparently, there was a significant storm somewhere far out in the Pacific Ocean, but the ripple effects of the storm were now hitting the island. I didn't notice anything out of the ordinary when I first started my walk, because the sun was out and it looked like a perfectly beautiful, calm, and predictable day. But once I reached the shore, I was completely shaken out of my serene predictability. I had never seen anything like this in my quiet, peaceful, beach cove. It was the most dramatic, out of control, and even terrifying yet beautiful surf I had ever seen. The waves were reaching inland and crashing over all barriers built as boundaries to keep the water at bay. The wind was blowing and the palm trees were bending. In one part of the cove, there are cliffs that are probably as high as a football field is long and the waves and surf reached all the way to the top.

Everything about this scene was both terrifying and beautiful at the same time. It was one of those moments when you realize that you are small and the earth is big and you could be swallowed up in an instant. The predictable became the out of control.

God was reminding me of the whole of who He is. We should never conclude that His serenity is slumber or that His patience is passivity. He is gentle, and He is fierce. He came as a vulnerable baby, but He's returning as a victorious King.

The same God who exhorts us to awake and come out of our stupor and slumber and recognize the hour we live in is the same God who tells us to "be still" and know that He is God and that we are to rest in Him and tarry with Him as He waits for the prodigals to come home.

> Awake, O Sleeper, and arise from the dead, and Christ will shine on you. (Ephesians 5:14)

> Therefore stay awake—for you do not know when the master of the house will come, in the evening, or at midnight, or when the rooster crows, or in the morning—lest he come suddenly and find you asleep. And what I say to you I say to all: Stay awake. (Mark 13:35–37)

> Be still, and know that I am God. I will be exalted among the nations; I will be exalted in the earth! (Psalm 46:10)
>
> Take my yoke upon you and learn from me, for I am gentle and lowly in heart, and you will find rest for your souls. (Matthew 11:29)
>
> For this my son was dead, and is alive again; he was lost, and is found. And they began to celebrate. (Luke 15:24)

The day is coming when the perfect justice of God will be decreed regarding the shedding of the innocent blood of the unborn. From our human perspective, we can only imagine that day as fierce and terrifying and full of dread and the fear of the Lord. But I believe if we truly had God's perspective and His vantage point, we would perceive that even this judgment and wrath is going to be a beautiful thing to behold.

Living in this world, none of us have ever witnessed perfect justice, nor do we have enough clarity in our own hearts and minds to discern how passionate God is for truth, righteousness, and justice. Our hearts and minds are so clouded by our ever-changing culture that we can't even muster a righteous indignation for the smorgasbord of new perversions we get exposed to every day.

I'm so comforted in the knowledge that God is a perfect and righteous judge. Aren't you? He is perfect in all His judgments, and His understanding is inscrutable. (Isaiah 40:28)

> Oh the depth of the riches and wisdom and knowledge of God! How unsearchable are his judgments and how inscrutable his ways! (Romans 11:33)

Our God, who is a righteous judge, is also a Father who is full of compassion and does not desire that any should perish.

> The Lord is not slow to fulfill his promise as some count slowness, but is patient toward you, not wishing that any should perish, but that all should reach repentance. (2 Peter 3:9)

> For God so loved the world that He gave his only begotten Son that whoever believes in Him shall not perish, but have eternal life. For God did not send the Son into the world to judge the world, but that the world might be saved through Him. (John 3:16–17)

This is the good news! Father God tarries and holds back His righteous judgments so that we might choose Him. God has sent a Savior into the world. He not only made a provision for us to be saved from the wrath to come but He also makes us one of His beloved children. He is preparing a new heaven and a new earth as our home for us for all eternity. And in that heavenly home, there is no more mourning or crying or pain (Revelation 21:4). Everything is made new and everything is perfect forever! There is no downside in this deal. It is the compassion and love of our Heavenly Father and our kind Savior, Jesus Christ, that went to great lengths to make a way for us to be delivered from our sin and to be healed from all our brokenness.

As I close out this book, I want to thank you for persevering through to the end and giving thought and consideration to the things I've written. I pray that your heart and mind will receive the good seed that has been planted and that you will allow it to bear good Kingdom fruit in your life.

Go Deeper Still

Lastly, I want to reiterate that if you have an abortion-wounded heart, I hope you engaged in the healing exercises and that you have experienced a measure of the healing power and presence of Jesus Christ. I recognize that not everyone who reads this book will be able to attend a Deeper Still retreat. However, this book is not intended to be a substitute for a full retreat. Some areas of healing and restoration can only be addressed within a healing community.

The mission of Deeper Still is to raise up leaders who will start a Deeper Still chapter in their area. There are millions of abortion-wounded souls around this country and the world. We want to see them all find healing and lasting freedom. Will you join us in a great prayer initiative to see this healing movement spread throughout the earth? If the Holy Spirit has been tugging at your heart to become one of those movement leaders, we want to hear from you.

Until all are healed,
KAREN A. ELLISON, Founder/President

You can find more information about Deeper Still on our website: www.GoDeeperStill.org

Deeper Still: Our Ministry Philosophy

Our Mission

The mission of Deeper Still is "to multiply ministry teams who bring healing and lasting freedom to abortion-wounded hearts."

To Multiply: We implement strategies of multiplication, not addition, wherever possible because:

- There are 1.1 million documented abortions in the US each year.
- There are 42 to 50 million abortions in the world each year.
- It is estimated that 70% of American women who have abortions identify themselves as Christians, so it is a huge pastoral care issue in the local church.

Our long-term growth strategy includes five primary channels through which to multiply our ministry.

- Starting a Deeper Still chapter as its own non-profit entity
- Starting a Deeper Still chapter in churches as part of their women's & men's ministries
- Starting a Deeper Still chapter in a pregnancy resource center as a part of their post-abortion ministry
- Through partnerships with existing mission agencies, churches, and other ministry movements
- Through the worldwide web by our Deeper Still Virtual Retreats conducted by our Virtual Missionary Ministry Team members

Ministry teams: Our ministry staff and volunteers are more productive and effective when they are placed in ministry teams and in community with one another.

Healing and lasting freedom is:

- **Evangelistic** – We ensure that our retreat participants and volunteers have been introduced to Jesus Christ, who is the Savior and Healer.
- **Spiritually Transforming** – As our participants fully engage in the spiritual legal work and prayer ministry we lead them through, they are transformed spiritually and emotionally. They are set free from guilt, shame, and pain.
- **Deep** – God's healing power does a quick work when He is allowed to do a deep work.

- **Lasting** – When our participants experience spiritual and emotional transformation, and then live it out in a healthy Christian community, their healing is deep and lasting.
- **Holy Spirit Led** – It is Jesus Christ who heals through the empowerment and leading of the Holy Spirit.
- **Preferred Approach** – We believe the best approach, whenever possible, is to facilitate this healing process in a weekend retreat or a similar sequestered environment.
- **To abortion-wounded hearts** – The women who've had abortions and the fathers of those children are the primary focus. However, abortion wounds also extend to family, friends, and others who participated in the abortions, such as medical professionals, clergy, and counselors.

Deeper Still Ministry Philosophy

The Deeper Still Ministry Philosophy can be visualized as a four-sided box describing our purpose, practices, and boundaries. These include our Mission, Guiding Principles, Central Ministry Focus, and Permeating Culture. These have been defined in order to bring clarity to the mission of Deeper Still. It allows our leaders to empower people within these clearly defined boundaries and brings alignment around our ministry philosophy rather than methodology.

Our Guiding Principles

- **Word-Based & Spirit-Empowered** – The Word of God revealed by the Holy Spirit is what brings the revelation of Jesus Christ, as the Redeemer and the Healer. Therefore, the teaching of the Scriptures and the empowerment and leading of the Holy Spirit are both fully and intentionally embraced.
- **Prayer & Worship Saturated** – Because we are a Christ-centered ministry, our foundation of prayer and worship both precedes and exceeds the breadth of our ministry activities. We saturate prayer and worship into every aspect of what we do.
- **Healing Differentiated** – Healing and lasting freedom can only be found in the stripes, blood, and sufficiency of the cross of Jesus Christ. This belief differentiates our ministry methods from other models that rely primarily on traditional counseling or therapy.
- **Team Led** – Believing that there is strength in multi-gifted team members and in the voice of multiple leaders, we are committed to a paradigm of team leadership under a gifted peer leader who is also an organizational leader with a vision for multiplication.
- **Identities Restored** – The consequences of abortion are systemic and can damage and redefine core identity issues for both women and men. Therefore, healing and lasting freedom

can only be secured when a person's God-designed identity is restored.

- **Environments Prepared** – We believe that the most conducive environment for healing wherever possible includes where God's presence and peace are invited and honored; physical and emotional safety; beauty; comforts; privacy; and the use of tangible symbols to represent spiritual realities.
- **Diversity Respected** – The abortion-wounded heart can be found in all social, economic, racial, cultural, gender, educational, and religious strata. We are intentional to reach into all of these strata (as God leads) and to culturally adapt our strategies and methods wherever possible.
- **Advocacy Affirmed** – The evidence of healing includes the freedom to speak and to act. Advocacy has unique forms of expression, according to the individual. But everyone is strongly encouraged to walk out the fruit of their healing through love and good deeds.
- **Ministry Resources** – A well-resourced ministry is more likely to be an effective organization. We embrace that, ultimately, the Lord is the provider of all our resources. Therefore, we must both pray and intentionally and effectively work to recruit the resources of people, strategy, and finances.

Our Central Ministry Focus

To Develop, Empower, and Release Healthy, Healing Leaders

- Develop: to Identify, Recruit, and Equip
- Empower: to Train, Mentor, and Apprentice
- Release: to Provide Opportunity & Promotion for Leadership into their ministry calling

We develop and provide venues for:

- Training on how to minister in Deeper Still
- Educating on the abortion-wounded heart
- Providing tools and resources
- Ministering healing and lasting freedom
- Advancing a lifestyle of prayer and worship

Our Permeating Culture

A Culture of Health and Community

- Healthy Leaders and Team Members
- Growing in spiritual, emotional, and relational health
- Become contributing members of a healthy team culture
- Healthy Retreat Participants – Men & Women
- Living in the light of the truth
- Free from guilt and shame

- Spiritually reconciled with their aborted children
- At peace with their redemptive grieving
- Walking in health and purity in their relationships
- Have the expectation for restoration in their life
- Gain their sense of destiny and find their voice
- Free to worship God with a whole heart
- Find their place in the Christian community

Community

For men and women to be restored back into authentic Christian fellowship and into the church, they need to experience healthy, Christian community so that hope for community can be restored. The Deeper Still ministry team models a community of servant leadership that serves one another, defers to one another, submits to one another, and honors one another. This strength and humility restores hope to those wounded by jealousy, judgment, and rejection.